Spon's Grounds
Maintenance
Contract Handbook

Spon's Grounds Maintenance Contract Handbook

Ronald M. Chadwick

E. & F.N. SPON
An imprint of Chapman and Hall
LONDON • NEW YORK • TOKYO • MELBOURNE • MADRAS

UK	Chapman and Hall, 2–6 Boundary Row, London SE1 8HN
USA	Van Nostrand Reinhold, 115 5th Avenue, New York NY10003
JAPAN	Chapman and Hall Japan, Thomson Publishing Japan, Hirakawacho Nemoto Building, 7F, 1-7-11 Hirakawa-cho, Chiyoda-ku, Tokyo 102
AUSTRALIA	Chapman and Hall Australia, Thomas Nelson Australia, 480 La Trobe Street, PO Box 4725, Melbourne 3000
INDIA	Chapman and Hall India, R. Seshadri, 32 Second Main Road, CIT East, Madras 600 035

First edition 1990

© 1990 Ronald M. Chadwick

Typeset in 10/12pt Palatino by Mayhew Typesetting, Bristol
Printed in Great Britain by T.J. Press (Padstow) Ltd,
Padstow, Cornwall

ISBN 0 419 15160 5
0 442 31235 0 (USA)

British Library Cataloguing in Publication Data

Chadwick, R.M. (Roy M)
  Spon's grounds maintenance contract handbook
  1. Great Britain. Buildings. Grounds. Construction &
  maintenance. Standard costs
  I. Title
  635.9

ISBN 0–419–15160–5

Library of Congress Cataloging in Publication Data
Available

Contents

Preface

This is a practical book, intended for those at the sharp end of contract grounds maintenance in Local Authorities and similar establishments. It will be of use to those who have to arrange contracts as well as those who have to run them. Those members of Direct Labour Organizations who have now found themselves in the curious situation of having to tender for their own work should also find much to interest them within its pages.

In 1979, the author, a landscape superintendent in the new city of Milton Keynes, was invited to establish a landscape maintenance contract section, in order to take some of the pressure off an over-stretched Direct Labour Organization. It was necessary to arrange the contracts, survey the sites, write all the documentation, find suitable contractors, let the contracts and then run them. In that first year, four small contracts were operated with a total value of £48 000. The experiment was successful and was continued and extended until now, eleven years later, we are well past our 500th contract with about 85% of the total maintenance work being contracted out, to the annual value of around £1¼ million.

During that period of time, a great deal has been learned and much experience gained. This book is an attempt to pass some of that experience on to those who may now be in need of a little help, when placed in a similar situation.

Although certain basic principles and legal requirements will apply in any contractual situation, there are many ways in which the detailed work can be arranged. Local circumstances and conditions vary, as do the specific requirements of individual Authorities. In addition, there are certain obvious differences in the way in which a Local Authority is required to operate, compared with that of a Development Corporation and this has been recognized and taken into account.

Consequently, the information offered here is not intended to be regarded as the only right way to do the job, but as one way which has been well tried and tested over time and found to be well suited to the particular requirements for which it was devised. It is up to the reader to modify and adapt where necessary to suit his or her own particular requirements and those of their employing Authority.

I am grateful to the Milton Keynes Development Corporation, firstly, for giving me the opportunity to gain experience in what has proved to be a fascinating, enjoyable and worthwhile aspect of the landscape manager's job, and secondly, for allowing me to make use of the Milton Keynes Specification and other documents in the compilation of this book. To the many friends and colleagues, both within the Development Corporation and outside it, who have, over the years, provided advice and information whenever it has been needed, I am also deeply grateful. I am particularly indebted to my publisher and to Mr Brian Salter of Milton Keynes Development Corporation, for reading the original manuscript and pointing out a number of discrepancies and important omissions. Action taken as a result of their comments must surely have improved the general usefulness of the book.

Finally, it must be said that all opinions, expressions and recommendations in this book are my own and not necessarily those of the Milton Keynes Development Corporation and I need hardly add that any mistakes which may have inadvertently crept into these pages are likewise my own responsibility.

Ron Chadwick

Foreword

Soft landscape and its sensitive management is an increasing expectation. The Landscape Industry and the professions associated with it have been hesitant in picking up the gauntlet of maintenance.

Public service managers have always had a mission to deliver 'quality of life' and 'value for money'. Consistent with this tradition, Ron Chadwick picked up the gauntlet in the late '70s and embarked upon an adventure to harness a part of the entrepreneurial drive of the New City of Milton Keynes into a reliable and predictable force in landscape maintenance. That adventure is not yet over and there will be more lessons and new developments to reckon with.

The author has committed himself to print at a time when many will be facing up to the demands and implications of Compulsory Competitive Tendering. The book offers honest advice, tempered by over a decade of practical experience. Landscape managers should find confidence and comfort from its shared approach to a previously uncharted world.

B.R. Salter MA MIC For
Recreation Unit Manager
Milton Keynes Development Corporation

CHAPTER 1

The concept of contract grounds maintenance

1.1 CHANGING TIMES

The concept of contract grounds maintenance is not new. Many Local Authorities and Government Agencies have been operating with contract labour for some years. On the one hand we have the small rural Parish Council which arranges for a local man, perhaps a farmer, to cut the village green twice a year, often for a nominal sum. At the other extreme there is the Property Services Agency, responsible for the maintenance of airfields, military establishments and Government properties all over the country, with a highly organized system of contract landscape maintenance operating contracts worth, in total, many millions of pounds annually.

Inbetween these extremes there are those County, Borough and District Councils who employ contractors for specific landscape works of a one-off nature, as well as a few who are no strangers to some form of regular Grounds Maintenance Contract, having been involved in this type of operation for a number of years.

Traditionally, of course, the bulk of the landscape maintenance in our towns and cities has generally been carried out by the staffs of the Local Authorities concerned, whose Direct Labour Organizations (DLOs) may include parks staff, nurserymen, groundsmen, gardeners, foresters and arboriculturists as well as those employed in ancillary enterprises such as catering, cleaning and others.

Today, however, the situation is changing, as Local Authorities are now obliged to contract out a certain minimum proportion of their grounds maintenance under the terms of the Local Government Act, 1988. This has been a very unpopular piece of legislation with many Authorities, but one with which most of them are rapidly coming to terms.

Legislation notwithstanding, in recent years a number of Authorities have been considering the political, economic and government pressures of contracting out at least some of the work of their Parks Departments to the private sector.

1.2 POLITICAL CONSIDERATIONS

The political reasons need not concern us greatly here. Policy making is the province of our elected representatives and the author is not prepared to engage in that particular arena. Nevertheless, it is undeniable that, in recent years, considerable pressures have been applied by central government to encourage privatization of many of the services traditionally provided by Local Authorities. This has now culminated in the Act to which reference has already been made, the implications of which will be discussed in later pages. The work of the Parks Department must be considered especially vulnerable in this situation, in view of its high labour intensity and the large amounts of revenue money expended annually.

The question of whether to go out to tender, or to continue with the existing system of in-house landscape maintenance, has long been a difficult one to resolve. Many left-wing-dominated Authorities (and not a few others) see it as part of their duty to provide local employment in the form of Direct Labour Organizations and are averse to any proposals that run counter to this. In this, they have the support of the Unions, whose members are naturally opposed to anything which seems likely to endanger their livelihood. There are powerful economic arguments, however.

1.3 ECONOMIC REASONS

From the taxpayer's point of view, privatization has much to commend it, as there is no doubt that properly managed contract landscape maintenance can be cost effective. Savings of between a quarter and a third may be expected, with no loss of working standards. This does not imply that the private sector employees are necessarily more efficient or more zealous than their Local Authority counterparts, but is mainly due to the following factors.

1.3.1 Overheads

Many DLOs are subject to a level of general overhead which no private business could tolerate. Contractors do not have to pay to support expensive town halls, armies of clerical and administrative staff and all the pomp and regalia which so often accompanies local government. This one factor alone is often sufficient to preclude the possibility of any DLO from ever becoming cost effective, through no fault of its own. Unless some alternative method of accounting can be adopted, which produces an overhead rate based only on those charges actually incurred by the DLO in the performance of its duties, and which is acceptable to all parties concerned, the Parks Department can never compete on level terms with the private sector.

1.3.2 Flexibility

Contractors generally have a much greater level of flexibility in the manner in which they control their staff. Although they, like the rest of us, have to abide by the Health and Safety Act, Employment Act and all the many other Acts and Regulations relating to employment of staff, they are less restricted in their interpretation of the various conditions imposed. They are better able to hire and fire and can take on temporary staff at peak times for short periods, according to the needs of the day. They are in a better position to resist excessive demands from staff with regard to pay and working conditions, despite the fact that some of the better firms offer conditions of service which compare very favourably with those encountered in Local Government Service.

1.3.3 Incentives

It is possible for private companies to offer incentives to their staff which those in Local Government are often unable to provide and this encourages greater productivity and a quicker turn-over of the work load. These may take the form of bonus payments, opportunities for overtime working, transport to and from work, gifts of consumer goods for achievement of target dates and the like. Some of the larger companies may offer profit-sharing schemes to their permanent employees.

1.3.4   Competition

Nothing is more calculated to bring down prices than the element of competition. The landscape industry is operating in a highly competitive situation with many companies vying for the available business. The effect of this is for firms to constantly seek ways of improving the efficiency and cost effectiveness of their business in order to win contracts.

In this, small, local contractors are at an advantage, as they can operate with minimum overheads, and are often prepared to accept a smaller margin of profit than some of their larger competitors.

On the other hand, the larger firms can often effect economies of scale when handling the larger contracts which are beyond the capacity of smaller companies to undertake.

For these reasons, the private sector should usually be able to operate more competitively than the average DLO, so that, on economic grounds alone, there would seem to be an overwhelming argument in favour of using contractors, in preference to in-house maintenance of grounds. There are other considerations, however.

1.4   IN SUPPORT OF THE DLO

In the implementation of the Local Government Act, most authorities have restructured their DLO in such a way as to enable them to adopt a 'contractor' role and themselves tender for the work of their own Authority. Many of them have been successful in this (Chapter 12). Where this has not happened, the use of private contractors would appear to threaten redundancy of at least an equivalent number of Local Authority staff and, in some cases, even the eventual closure of the DLO entirely. There is a very good case against this, however.

In the first place, in order that a contract maintenance programme should operate successfully, we need good contractors, a good contract and good client management. These matters are dealt with at length in later chapters of this book; suffice it to say here that if the mix is right, all will be well. Unfortunately, the practical reality sometimes falls short of the theoretical ideal and it is well to be prepared for such an eventuality.

It can be reassuring to know that, if the worst happens, there is a back-up team ready to step in if required, in order to fill what would otherwise be an embarrassing void. This knowledge will also strengthen considerably the Authorities dealings with the contractor concerned.

Secondly, there are some aspects of grounds maintenance which may be considered to be inappropriate for inclusion in a maintenance contract. These may include ticket selling, booking of pitches and other recreational facilities, promotion of special floral displays, Britain in Bloom, Best Kept Village Competitions and others.

Then there is the problem of the quick response. We are all familiar with the situation where unexpected urgent work is required, where an immediate response is vital. It may be a question of making good the effects of a bad spate of vandalism, or the 'VIP's visit', where the route has to be checked and quickly tidied up at the last minute. It is not always possible to obtain the immediate response required in these circumstances from the maintenance contractor as his or her staff are not under our direct control.

There is a very good argument for retaining a part of the DLO as a small but viable unit to cover the sort of eventualities described above. The 'private contractor versus DLO' argument has been running for years, and is likely to continue for years to come. It is suggested that the conflict is not as great as normally imagined, as there is a role for both types of organizations in most Parks Departments.

1.5 THE TRAINING OF GARDENERS

The question of training is one that needs to be considered also. Many of today's skilled gardeners owe their craftsman status to the training they have received while in the employ of Local

Authorities. They will have benefited from short courses in particular craft skills as well as from day release, on full pay, for the purpose of obtaining more general qualifications in horticulture and allied subjects, in order to further their careers. This has been going on for many years and it is largely due to the encouragement and assistance provided by the employers that we have a pool of trained, skilled and qualified gardeners available today. If the DLOs were to disappear, or to be drastically curtailed, it is difficult to see who is to continue this support. The contractors are unlikely to provide such facilities as, apart from the financial considerations, they would not wish to lose the services of their staff, on a regular day-release basis, throughout the major part of the year. Where then, is the industry's future trained staff to come from?

The colleges may have a part to play in this, as by restructuring their courses it might be possible to compress a whole year's day release into a few weeks' intensive block training during the winter period, when the average contractor might be more amenable to releasing staff for training, at a time of year when he or she is less busy.

If this could be supported by some sort of training grant from central government, financed in part by a training levy arranged on a per capita basis, so much the better.

The above scheme, supplemented by the continued efforts of those DLOs remaining, albeit perhaps at a lower level, would ensure the continuing flow of trained staff for future generations of gardeners.

CHAPTER 2

Some basic considerations

Before considering some of the more basic aspects of contract grounds maintenance, it might be useful to look briefly at the Act which has been largely responsible for its instigation.

2.1 THE LOCAL GOVERNMENT ACT 1988

The Local Government Act is a comprehensive one, which embodies such diverse matters as the provision of public services, financial regulations, dog registration, publicity and the prohibitions of the promotion of homosexuality, and is designed to limit, control and regulate the actions of Local Authorities in these and other spheres of action. The particular section which concerns us here is, of course, that which deals with the maintenance of grounds by Local Authorities.

The following brief résumé of the Act, in so far as it applies to Local Authority grounds maintenance, is not intended to replace a detailed reading and study of the Act itself. In all cases, reference should be made to the official publication by HMSO, with professional advice being taken on its interpretation in any particular cicumstances.

The Act requires that a 'defined authority' shall undertake certain 'defined activities' only if they can do so competitively. The Act applies throughout England, Scotland and Wales, including island authorities where appropriate; it does not apply to Northern Ireland.

A defined authority includes:

1. Local Authorities
2. Police Authorities
3. Fire and Civil Defence Authorities
4. Metropolitan County Passenger Transport Authorities
5. Waste Disposal Authorities
6. Education Authorities
7. Scottish Water Development Boards
8. The Scottish Special Housing Association

Local Authorities are further defined as:

1. County Councils
2. District Councils
3. London Borough Councils
4. Parish Councils
5. Community Councils
6. Council of the Isles of Scilly

and in Scotland:

1. Regional Island or District Councils
2. Joint Boards or Committees

Defined activities include:

1. Collection of refuse
2. Cleaning of buildings
3. Other cleaning
4. School, welfare and other catering
5. Maintenance of ground
6. Repair and maintenance of vehicles

There is a certain amount of overlap between the authorities responsible for certain activities and between certain of the activities themselves. The Act makes clear what is required in these cases. There are also certain exceptions identified and these include major emergency work and the regular maintenance of grounds which are the subject of scientific research or conservation.

In order to prove its competitiveness, an Authority is required to compete with the private sector for a proportion of its grounds maintenance work. A minimum of 20% must have been offered for competition during the first year, with a further 20% in each successive year. Contracts must be prepared and specifications drawn up. At least three private contractors must be given the opportunity to tender for the work on each occasion with the Authority's own DLO preparing a bid on exactly the same terms as required of the private contractor. Only if the DLOs tender proves to be the most favourable, may it proceed with the work, which must then be performed in strict accordance with the specifications. In these circumstances the DLO will be operating under a 'works contract'.

An Authority may also bid for appropriate work with another Authority, although the initiating Authority has the right to refuse such a bid if it so wishes. Work carried out by a DLO for another Authority is classed as 'functional work' and does not become the subject of a works contract.

The conditions under which contracts may be offered are precisely defined, as is the method by which selection of tenderers is to be made. There is a choice of selection from an approved list of contractors or of open tendering involving the placing of advertisements in local newspapers and other appropriate journals.

Throughout the whole procedure, the Authority must ensure that nothing is done which restricts, distorts or prevents competition. Accurate and comprehensive accounts must be kept and reports prepared and these are liable to inspection and audit.

The Act provides for sanctions to be imposed on Authorities who fail to comply with the requirements of the legislation and these could ultimately lead to the taking away of an Authority's powers to carry out the type of work for which the sanctions have been applied.

From this brief and very much oversimplified description of the Local Government Act, it will be seen that the purpose of the Act is not necessarily to introduce private contractors to the detriment of the DLO, but rather, to encourage the DLO to become more cost conscious and to operate more efficiently. If it can prove its ability in this respect, it will have little to fear from the competition.

When the Act was first introduced, some Authorities, seeing the Act as a threat, appear to have acted in such a way as to make it difficult for the private contractor to compete on level terms. Such ploys as charging excessive amounts for copies of the specification, writing into the terms of contract the sort of conditions with which the average private contractor would find it very difficult to comply, or, at best, excessively expensive, are prohibited by the Act. These negative attitudes are to be deplored; they are as unnecessary as they are undesirable. Such instances, although known, are in the minority, the majority of Local Authorities having taken the reasonable view, often to be pleasantly surprised at the eventual outcome.

Accepting, then, that landscape contractors are to be involved in the work of the Parks Department, how are we to go about it?

2.2   GAINING EXPERIENCE

If there is no previous experience of contract maintenance in the Department, wise managers would do well to first examine the experience of others. They should seek out those who are already operating with contractors and examine their methods, especially those nearest to them, as their problems are likely to be similar. It is unlikely that any reasonable request for information will be refused, indeed most landscape managers appear to welcome the opportunity to discuss their work with fellow horticulturists.

Much useful information may be gained from examination of the ways in which other people operate and it is often possible to adapt other people's ideas and build them into our own system. The key word here is 'adapt', for it is a mistake to imagine that a complete system of contract management can simply be picked up and transplanted elsewhere, without modification. We must be selective and examine each new idea as it comes along, accepting some, rejecting others. No two places are the same and no two Authorities operate under the same conditions. What works in one place may not work in another.

Would-be contract managers will be aware of their brief and familiar with their own particular circumstances. It is up to them to obtain the best possible information to enable them to select and put together a contract system that is likely to run smoothly and efficiently and that will be acceptable to their Authority.

2.3   TERM CONTRACTS

There are three main ways in which a term contract may be arranged. These are:

1. Fixed price term contract
2. Variable price term contract
3. Unit rate term contract

2.3.1 Fixed price contracts

This type of contract requires the tenderer to state his or her total price for the whole of the works required, for the whole of the contract period. Sufficient information is provided in the tender package for the contractor to do this, i.e. full details of all work required, quantified in a manner which will enable an accurate assessment of cost to be made. The contractor will be paid the exact amount of his or her tender, for which he or she will be required to perform the whole of the works described in the contract documentation.

This is the simplest type of contract to administer although it allows for little flexibility. Any additional work which might arise will require to be separately negotiated; contract payments cannot be reduced provided that the whole of the work has been performed in accordance with the specification.

2.3.2 Variable price contracts

These are similar to the above, but all work done is measured and payment is made for work actually completed up to the date of the invoice. This allows for adjustment of the work load to suit local conditions with variable payments based on actual performance. It is necessary for the contract documents to include a priced Bill of Quantities with this type of contract in order that the appropriate payments may be calculated from time to time.

2.3.3 Unit rate contracts

With this type of contract the contractor submits his or her unit rates for each operation on a Bill of Quantities or Schedule of Rates and all work is ordered as required by the Supervising Officer. Payment is made on the basis of work performed. This allows maximum control of the work by the client but also requires maximum attention to the site by the Supervising Officer as the contractor will do nothing until he receives an order or instructions for specific items of work. Chapter 10 describes the Schedule of Rates which can usefully be employed for this type of contract.

2.3.4 Basis of the specification

In the operation of the first two types of contract the amount of work required may be specified in two ways. This can best be explained by considering an example based on grass-cutting.

The specification might call for the grass to be cut on 18 occasions throughout the season. This means that the contractor must go through the motions of grass-cutting 18 times, whether necessary or not. If the growing conditions are such as to require more than 18 cuts, any additional operations over and above this number will have to be separately ordered and paid for in addition to the normal contract payments. Either way, somebody loses out: either the contractor who may have to perform unnecessary grass cuts when there is no grass to cut (and the client who has to pay for them) or the client who may be faced with additional expenditure if extra cuts are required. This is an operation-based specification, i.e. one where the exact number of operations are clearly stated and priced accordingly.

Under the alternative, performance based, specification we might say something like:

'the grass shall be maintained at a height not exceeding 50 mm throughout the growing season'.

This puts the onus on the contractor to estimate, using his or her experience of previous working, the number of cuts likely to be required and to tender accordingly. The contractor may gain or lose, depending on whether the following season is conducive to grass growth or not; either way the client can be assured that whatever cuts are required will be carried out and a simple visual inspection will be all that is necessary to ensure that the work is up to date.

The choice of which of these two methods should be used is largely a matter of personal preference and local custom, bearing in mind the experience and reliability of the contractors likely to be available and the cost implications involved. It is permissible to combine both methods into the one specification if desired, as in the example offered in the Appendix to this book.

2.3.5 Size and timing of contracts

The contract area may be a park, a cemetery, a housing area or any other such landscaped grounds which it is desired to maintain. It may be a combination of these elements, not necessarily physically connected or of the same type. It may even be the whole of the available maintenance, although this is not recommended in the majority of cases.

If it is decided to put out the whole of the works in one single package, the total enterprise is dependent upon the performance of a single contractor, and if the contractor does not come up to expectations, all is lost. It is far better to divide up the estate into a number of separate contracts, some small, some large, so that a number of different contractors are operating simultaneously, each in their own particular area. This will render less serious the effect of poor or unsatisfactory performance on the part of any one of them. It will also enable specialist contractors to be used, e.g. on sports grounds, while reserving the less exacting work for the more general type of contractor.

It will be found that with contracts of different sizes, the number of interested contractors will be increased. Large contracts, perhaps with an annual value in excess of £50 000 will attract medium to large sized regional companies, while the smaller jobs will be within the range of small local firms – horses for courses.

While the annual value of a contract will obviously depend on its size, it is perhaps not so obvious that the length of the contract may also influence its price. Long-term contracts tend to be cheaper than a succession of shorter ones.

A maintenance contract may run for one year or several years. The smaller contracts can often be successfully offered to local firms on a one or two year basis. Larger contracts, especially if they are offered to companies that are not based in the area, may need to be arranged for longer periods.

Contractors generally do not favour short-term contracts, and it will be found that the larger companies in particular will not usually consider anything under three years and preferably five or more. This is perhaps not unreasonable when it is considered that the contractor may wish to purchase new machinery in order to operate the new contract and will seek to recover his or her capital investment over the life of the contract. If the contract is of short duration this may not be possible and there is no guarantee that further work will be available for the equipment in subsequent years.

As new equipment is more efficient and less costly to maintain contractors will be able to reduce their operating costs and thus make their tenders more competitive.

In general, those areas where large areas of grass-cutting are involved should be arranged as large contracts of at least three years duration, while those which are more labour intensive may form the basis of a number of smaller ones, running perhaps for one or two years only.

Some thought should be given to when the contract is to commence and opinions differ on this matter.

There is much to be said in favour of a start on 1 April, or the first Monday in that month. By arranging the contract year to coincide with the financial year the accounting is simplified and payments throughout the year are most easily related to annual budgets. The site survey work necessary to produce the contract drawings and the landscape quantities is best done during the summer months when the weather is likely to be most favourable to this operation and this allows for production of the drawings and Bills of Quantities in the autumn in time for preparation of the contract during the winter period, in anticipation of a spring start.

The main objection to this, however, is that where grass-cutting forms a major part of the contract work, the contractor is likely to be required to input maximum resources almost from the beginning of the contract period. This may occasion financial and organizational problems for the contractor during the vital first few weeks of the contract before he or she has had an opportunity to become familiar with the site. The position may be further aggravated if the site has not been left in 'running order' by the previous contractor as there will be little opportunity to catch up with any preparatory work before grass-cutting commences.

Many Authorities and some contractors favour a contract start date at the beginning of January, which allows a gradual build-up of activity before the main part of the work commences. The financial implications are such that contractors are likely to be in a better position to regulate their cash flow at this time of the year and can reasonably expect to receive the first of their interim payments in time to assist in financing the major build-up of activity towards the grasscutting season. Contractors who are involved in major planting contracts, however, may find some difficulty in providing the required resources for a new contract while the bulk of their staff is involved in establishment work during the planting season.

In general it will be seen that the decision regarding the contract start date may be based on a number of considerations and they include:

1. The availability of contract drawings and quantities
2. The nature of the contract – whether or not the bulk of the work is summer orientated (e.g. grass maintenance)
3. The financial standing of the eligible tenderers
4. The present workloads of the eligible tenderers (if known)

Reference has already been made to 'small' contracts and 'large' ones and these descriptions will recur in succeeding pages. These terms are difficult to define as one person's 'small' is another's 'large' and vice versa. Within the covers of this book, however, 'small' can be taken to refer to contracts with annual values of £10 000–£50 000, which may be the subject of short-term contracts up to two years' duration, perhaps with continuity.

Anything over £50 000 per annum will be described as a large contract and will normally run for at least three years.

Any work estimated at less than £10 000 per annum is probably best dealt with on a schedule of rates basis, as described in a later chapter, although successful term contracts can be operated in the £5000–£10 000 range if desired, using small local contractors.

2.3.6 Continuity contracts

In order to make short-term contracts more attractive, consideration may be given to the negotiation of continuity contracts, to follow on when the main contracts are completed. This will enable the contractor to continue the work for a further year, or years, without the need to retender. The length of the continuity should not be more than that of the contract itself and it will be necessary to provide for such an option in the original contract document. The price will be the original tender price adjusted by means of price indices or other acceptable method.

The continuity should not be automatic, but granted at the discretion of the client, in the light of previous performance and current market trends.

2.4   A GRADUAL TRANSITION

It is not advisable to attempt to change over the whole of the maintenance from DLO maintenance to contract maintenance in the first year. In addition to the large number of redundancies which this might entail, the problems of contract management would be met head-on by staff who were probably not ready to deal with them.

It is far better to start in a small way, by contracting out some 20–25% of the work initially and building up, over a period of four or five years, until all of the total maintenance is eventually placed with the private sector. This would enable hands-on experience of contract management and supervision to be gained gradually, while also allowing for the build-up of a pool of approved contractors. The workload of the contract section would then be distributed over a number of years, with contracts becoming renewable year by year, instead of all at the same time. Any natural wastage of DLO staff that occurred would also go some way towards reducing the number of redundancies which would eventually become necessary. The Local Government Act recognizes this by requiring only a minimum of 20% of the available work to be offered for competition in the initial year, with a further 20% in each succeeding year.

The DLO should be reduced each year, as more and more of the maintenance is transferred to the contract section. It should not be dismantled completely, however, the aim being to reduce it to a small, efficient, viable unit with its own maintenance areas to look after, on a permanent basis.

Here we have a problem, however, as under the present terms of the Act, in the fifth year the final 20% must be offered to the private sector, thus implying that the whole of the works would then be privatized, leaving nothing for the DLO to do and removing the justification for any further retention of Local Authority staff other than those involved in the supervision of the contracts for the client section.

It is to be hoped that a way out of this dilemma may be found but, unless the Act is subsequently amended, it is difficult to see how the DLO can be retained after the fifth year. Of course, the DLO, if acting as a contractor, can be retained indefinitely, so long as it continues to win contracts in fair competition with the private sector, but this is not the same thing as is advocated here.

Accordingly, the following section is written somewhat tongue in cheek and is offered as something which would be eminently desirable if the Local Government Act, when the time comes, should permit of it.

2.5 THE ROLE OF THE DLO

The role of the DLO, in these circumstances, would be:

1. To carry out any particular duties which, for one reason or another, the Authority might wish to retain under its direct control.
2. To maintain a standard of work on its own particular areas of responsibility, against which the performance of the contractors might be compared.
3. To provide a cost base for the preparation of estimates and other prices.
4. To investigate new techniques and developments and evaluate them with a view to their possible future use in the maintenance, generally.
5. To deal with urgent one-off jobs, as they occur, where a quick response is required.
6. To act as a temporary life line in the event of failure of a contract, should this ever occur.

The size of the DLO should be as small as possible, consistent with the unit remaining viable and cost effective. If it is desired to allow the DLO itself to tender for contract maintenance, this should be a consideration in determining the size of the unit and its consequent regular maintenance commitment.

It is earnestly hoped that it may be possible to retain a small section of the DLO for the purpose of carrying out the functions outlined above, but as the law stands at the time of writing, this will not be possible.

CHAPTER 3

Preparing the ground — surveying

3.1 THE NEED FOR INFORMATION

When preparing a contract for grounds maintenance, whether it be a public park, housing estate, playing fields or any other form of landscape, a major consideration will be that of providing the essential information. Unlike the Parks Manager and staff, who will be familiar with every nook and cranny of the sites in their charge, the contractor, initially, will know nothing. He or she will need to be told where the site is, of what it consists and to be provided with some form of quantitative information.

This information will be provided in the tender package and will be used by the contractor to calculate his or her tender price. It will be presented in the form of drawings and a Bill of Quantities.

3.2 CONTRACT DRAWINGS

The contract drawings should be comprehensive, accurate, up to date and of an appropriate scale for the type of work portrayed. It is unlikely that any existing drawings will be found to be suitable and in the majority of cases it will be necessary to prepare them specially for the contract.

The drawings should show all the landscape features which are subject to the contract, uncluttered with extraneous detail. The contract boundary should be clearly marked and the principal access routes indicated. Grass areas can be shown dotted and various forms of shading used to indicate shrub and other

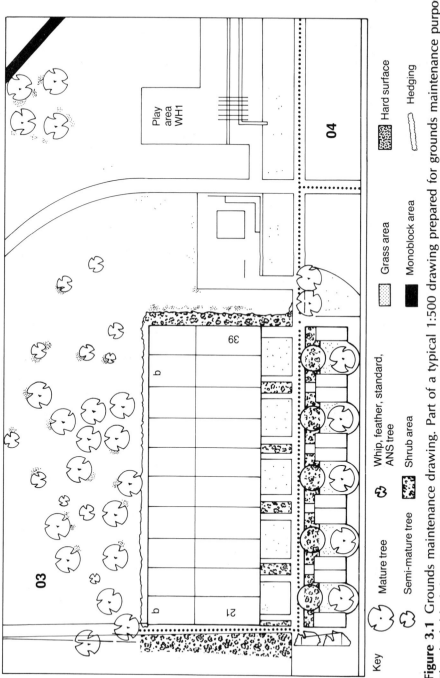

Figure 3.1 Grounds maintenance drawing. Part of a typical 1:500 drawing prepared for grounds maintenance purposes. The thick black line (top right) is the contract boundary; the dotted lines are card boundaries; 03 and 04 are card numbers

Key

Mature tree

Semi-mature tree

Whip, feather, standard, ANS tree

Shrub area

Grass area

Monoblock area

Hard surface

Hedging

planted areas. British Standard BS 1/92 includes examples of conventional signs for use in construction drawing and these should be used where possible. All non-standard signs should be included in a key on each drawing. Buildings should be indicated in outline only. It is not usually necessary to indicate slope, or elevation, although restrained use of hachures may be employed where it is desired to show steep banks.

The chosen scale will depend on the size and complexity of the site and the number of features to be included. For general purposes a scale of 1:500 will be found suitable and at this scale it is possible to plot the position of individual trees (Figure 3.1).

If it is desired to show a complicated planting layout in detail it may be necessary to use a scale of 1:200. Large areas of open space may well require 1:1000 or 1:1250.

If landscape or engineering drawings are available, at the appropriate scale, these may be used as a basis for the preparation of the contract drawings. By tracing the principal features a base map can be prepared, on which the required details can then be inserted.

As an alternative to the traditional methods of producing drawings, a computer-aided draughting system, although expensive to install, will produce a very professional drawing, using digitized techniques. A particular advantage of this type of system is the ease with which alterations and modifications may be made at any time. The process may be likened to the alteration of text on a word processor and a modified drawing may be produced in minutes, which might otherwise take several days to redraw by hand.

The Ordnance Survey is now producing digitized maps which can be tailored to the particular requirements of any client. They may incorporate as much or as little detail as is required and can be produced at any appropriate scale. At the time of writing, availability is limited to a relatively small area of the country, but as this system becomes more widespread it is likely to prove a valuable source of base maps for the purpose described here.

In the event that no suitable drawings can be found for preparation of a base map, it will be necessary to send out a survey team to conduct the necessary work on site. Some field work will be required in either eventuality in order to ascertain the present layout and to plot the individual landscape details, as it is important that the drawings reflect the current situation rather than the as-built one, which may be quite different. The survey team will also gather the information from site for preparation of the landscape schedules, required for compiling the Bills of Quantities, and this will go hand in hand with the preparation of the drawings.

3.3 LANDSCAPE SCHEDULES

The Landscape Schedule represents an attempt to quantify those elements of the landscape which are specifically mentioned in the contract. The contractor will need to know the area of grass to be cut, the number of trees and shrubs to be maintained, the length of hedging to be trimmed and similar matters, in order to prepare a realistic tender.

Here we have a problem. The established landscape is not static. It is a living, growing thing, constantly in a state of change. Plants die, are vandalized or even stolen. At some point of time the half standard becomes a standard and the standard tree assumes larger proportions. A plant count is rather like a stock-taking exercise: it is only correct on the day it is actually done. By the following day it may be different.

As the quantities will have been prepared at least several months before the first day of the contract, there can be no guarantee that the numbers on that day will be exactly as stated in the Schedule. In the intervening period, some newly planted trees may have died, or conversely, more may have been planted. Minor landscape modifications may have been made, including perhaps the seeding down of a shrub bed, the removal of a length of hedge or the realignment of a footpath. That is what maintenance is all about. In consequence, any quantities stated can only be regarded as approximate ones and this should be made clear in the specification.

3.4 FIELD WORK

The survey team, consisting of two people, will visit every part of the contract area gathering information for the drawings and the Landscape Schedule. They should work systematically, taking a section at a time, and will identify, measure and count all relevant features as they come to them.

Measurements may be taken with a measuring wheel and recorded as accurately as the measuring equipment will allow. This will normally be to the nearest tenth of a metre or, if an imperial wheel is used, to the nearest foot. Irregular areas will be divided into rectangles and triangles and appropriate measurements taken to enable the shape to be plotted and its area found by computation.

If a base map is available, the measurements can be marked directly on to this as they are taken, along with other information in note form, which will enable a comprehensive drawing to be made on return to the office. Otherwise, the information will be recorded in a field notebook, or on sheets attached to a clipboard.

While areas can be worked out at a later date, any individual counts must, obviously, be made in the field and these should be accurately recorded. Totalling up will be carried out when all of the site has been surveyed and can most conveniently be done indoors. Rounding up of quantities should be left until the final totals have been prepared.

3.5   LANDSCAPE FEATURES

The landscape features that need to be recorded will depend on the nature of the contract. It is likely, however, that most, if not all of the following will be required.

3.5.1   Grass

The total grass area should be subdivided according to the mowing regime. The first distinction may be between fine grass and rough. (These terms should be defined in the specification.) Broadly speaking, fine grass areas will be cylinder mown to a fairly high standard, while rough grass areas will be cut less frequently with rotary or flail mowers.

Further subdivisions are possible, e.g. gangmowing, triple mowing, mowing with pedestrian-operated machines, etc. If separate subtotals are provided for each of these categories, the tenderer will be better able to provide accurate pricings.

3.5.2 Rose beds

Two basic subdivisions according to the method of pruning, i.e. hybrid tea and floribunda. Separate area totals will be required for each.

3.5.3 Herbaceous beds

The total area of herbaceous planted beds may be split between perennials, bedding and bulbs, as appropriate.

3.5.4 Shrub beds

One total figure will probably cover the shrub bed area although sub-totals based on species and/or method of pruning may be prepared if required.

3.5.5 Hard surface

This is the area of paving and other hard areas which it is desired to maintain in weed-free condition, probably by the use of total weed killers.

3.5.6 Grass edging

The length of grass edging will be specified.

3.5.7 Hedging

If hedge trimming is required it will be necessary to state the total length of hedge to be trimmed. If all the hedges on site are of similar type and height, and are to be maintained in the same way throughout, it will be sufficient to provide a total length. It is likely that subtotals will be required, however, to take account of different treatments. These may be based on whether the hedge is to be trimmed on one side only, one side and top, two sides or two sides and top. Varying heights might have to be considered and large-leaved species such as laurel should be separately measured.

3.5.8 Trees

This will be a numerical count and the total may be broken down according to size, e.g. standards, advanced nursery stock, semi-mature, mature, etc. Alternatively, the divisions might be simply into two categories, staked trees and unstaked.

The above list is not intended to be exhaustive, nor will all the categories mentioned be required on every occasion. The required items will depend on the nature of the maintenance site and the specific requirements of the contract.

Other classifications will suggest themselves with regard to particular types of contract. For example, if the contract is for a sports ground, information will be needed with regard to the number of pitches or playing areas of different types.

In public parks, special features, where they affect the maintenance, should be noted. These may include rock gardens, water features, children's play areas and other such diverse elements of the landscape. It will be necessary to brief the survey team on each occasion so that they collect the appropriate information for each site.

3.6 RECORDING THE INFORMATION

After completing the field work it will be necessary to record and store the information that has been obtained, in order to preserve it for future reference and to facilitate the calculations that must be made. A convenient method of doing this involves the use of coloured record cards as illustrated in Figure 3.2.

The cards, of A4 size, are arranged in sets, each set relating to a complete maintenance area. The sets of cards may be stored in vertical files and if each set is a different colour from that of its neighbours, this will facilitate rapid identification as well as reducing the risk of a card being accidentally replaced in an incorrect set.

The number of cards in a set will vary depending on the size and complexity of the site. Cards are serially numbered within each set and each one carries all the information relating to a small section of the site. It will be found useful to indicate the boundaries of the card areas on the final drawings along with the card numbers. This can be seen in Figure 3.1 where card

Area Description	Size & Location		Trees			Grass		Plants & Shrubs
Position	Descpn	Size	Qty	Species	Size	edge m	cat.	Species
OPEN AREA BEHIND 1-39	GRASS	852m²	44	ACER PLATANOIDES	ANS	457	5	
HUNSTANTON WAY AND			31	TILIA CORDATA	ANS			
SURROUNDING PLAY AREA			9	SORBUS AUCUPARIA	ANS			
" "			4	ROBINIA PSEUDACACIA	STD			
SIDE OF 76 WALTON HEATH	GRASS	143m²	2	TILIA CORDATA	ANS	43	5	
" "	AG. HEDGE	145m						CRATAEGOS MONOGYNA / ROSA RUGOSA
PLAY AREA	PAVING	390m²						
REAR 1-19 HUNSTANTON	HEDGING 6'	45.0m						
" 21-39 "	HEDGING 6'	45.0m						
SIDE 39 "	SHRUB BED	44.0m²						CORNOS ALBA / PRUNUS LAUROCERASUS
" 80 "	SHRUB BED	68.5m²						"

Figure 3.2 Grounds record card. One of a set of nine survey cards prepared for a small housing estate. Compare with drawing in Figure 3.1

numbers are shown, the card boundaries being indicated by dotted lines.

The cards will be filled in with information collected by the survey team and reference to Figure 3.2 will show how this is done.

Each card will be headed with the name of the estate or maintenance area, the card number and date of compilation.

Column 1 gives an approximate location, usually a street address, while column 2 identifies the exact position. The information may be given in abbreviated form and use made of such terms as: front, back, side and the cardinal points N, E, S and W.

The next two columns are for surface areas, the first describing the type of surface, e.g. grass, shrub bed etc., and the second detailing the actual area (in square metres).

Columns 5, 6 and 7 are for trees and list the number, species and size respectively. Tree size is recorded by the use of terms such as STD (Standard), ANS (Advance Nursery Stock) and SM (Semi Mature).

The two narrow columns which follow are for grass, the first recording the length of grass edging in metres and the other the grass category, if applicable. The figure 5 which appears in this column in Figure 3.2 is an internal code for triple mowing.

The final column is used to record the species of shrubs and other plants and will be found particularly useful when plant replacements are being considered.

As each card is completed the totals are calculated and recorded on the reverse of the record card. Thus, in the example provided we would expect to see:

Grass, category 5	3664 m²
Grass edging	500 m
Hard surface	390 m²
Shrub beds	112.5 m²
Trees Std	4
ANS	86
Total	90
Hedging Cat 'B'	90 m

These card totals are then added together to produce final totals for the whole area and these are recorded on a separate summary card which is filed with each set. The summary cards provide the information for compiling the Landscape Schedules for the contracts.

If computer facilities are available it is well worth considering the possibility of storing all these records electronically. A suitable program would produce print-outs of any area, parts of area or combinations of areas, faster and with greater accuracy then by manual methods. Additions and updates would be facilitated and if cost information was input, estimates and pricings could be prepared with considerable savings of time. The initial cost of programming would be high, but once done, the operating cost would be small and the savings in time of speed, simplicity, accuracy and cost would be of major proportions. Computer packages are available commercially which carry out all these functions and if cost is not the prime consideration, much time may be saved by purchasing such a package 'off the shelf'.

3.7   AN ONGOING PROCESS

The survey process does not stop when all the maintenance areas have been recorded. Provision should be made for updating at regular intervals so that the drawings and the quantities may be kept up to date. An ongoing programme of site revisions, at perhaps three-year intervals, will be required if this is to be effective.

The time required for this will be small compared with the time needed for the original survey but it must not be overlooked if the contract information is to reflect a true picture of what is actually on site.

CHAPTER 4

Contractors

In any contract situation it is important to ensure that the right sort of contractor is employed and this is particularly relevant in relation to grounds maintenance contracts. Landscape contractors vary considerably with regard to the type of work they are equipped to do and the size of contract that they can perform. Consequently it is necessary to ensure that, as far as possible, the contractor is matched to the contract, if the best results are to be obtained.

4.1 SIZE OF CONTRACT FIRMS

Landscape contractors may be categorized by size and by the types of work in which they specialize. Dealing first with the size of the firm, three main groups of contractors may be distinguished. These are: small local contractors, regional firms and the large national companies. These divisions are not clear cut and there is considerable overlapping, but it is useful to consider these three groups in relation to the size and types of contract to be placed.

4.1.1 Small local contractors

The small local contractor is often a one-man concern, employing additional help on a casual basis when needed. It may be a family business, perhaps two brothers in partnership, or a father and son. Some of the more successful firms may employ up to about half a dozen operatives on a regular basis, but this is exceptional.

These firms often start out as small private garden contractors, widening their scope as they gain business experience. In most large towns, such firms abound, as a glance through the yellow pages of the local telephone directory will show. Many of them will be unsuitable for Local Government contract work, having only limited experience and perhaps lacking the necessary business awareness to deal with all but the simplest of jobs. The best of them are capable of producing work of a very high standard at extremely competitive prices and can usefully be employed on Schedule of Rates work as described in Chapter 10, as well as small maintenance contracts up to about £10 000 in value. Some guidance may be needed initially, particularly with regard to contractual matters and procedures, as this might be a new venture for them. Great care should be taken in selection of small local contractors in order to eliminate those who, for one reason or another, are unsuitable. Particular attention should be paid to their financial status and the position with regard to insurance and the payment of tax.

4.1.2 Regional firms

Regional firms will be able to undertake works of a more comprehensive nature and may be considered for contracts up to about £100 000 annual value, in some cases substantially more. These are well-established firms with considerable experience, probably employing upwards of a dozen permanent staff and operating within a radius of fifty or sixty miles from their home base. Many of them are prepared to go further afield and sometimes employ local firms as sub-contractors for such works. A contract manager will be employed, whose job it is to seek out new contracts and to supervise current contract work. If they do not actually employ a quantity surveyor they will certainly have access to such services when required, and will usually retain a solicitor to act for them in legal matters. They will be fully conversant with normal contract procedure and familiar with the standard forms of documentation.

There is no shortage of such regional companies in the southern part of England; the rest of the country as well as Wales and Scotland is perhaps not so well served, however. This situation might change as privatization of Local Government services gets under way.

4.1.3   Large national companies

These are the largest of the landscape companies with branches or subsidiaries in many parts of the country. Each branch will have its own manager and will often be expected to operate as an independant profit-making unit, although able to call on the resources of the whole company when required. They can handle the largest of contracts and exhibit a high degree of professionalism.

These companies tend to be somewhat more expensive than smaller firms because of their relatively high overhead costs, but their usefulness lies in their ability to undertake very large contracts and often, to carry out work of a specialized nature. They are unlikely to be attracted by anything under about £50 000 and most of them will only consider maintenance contracts of at least three or five years' duration.

4.2   TYPE OF WORK

As well as the broad size classifications described above, it is necessary to consider landscape contractors according to the type of work that they have to offer. Landscape or grounds maintenance covers a multitude of activities and not all firms are able to deal with every aspect of the business. It is therefore necessary to know the kind of work that particular contractors can offer and these can be roughly categorized as follows.

4.2.1   General landscape maintenance

The most useful type of firm will probably be the one who can offer a complete landscape service, which includes maintenance of grass, planted beds, shrubs, roses, small trees as well as litter collection and maintenance of paths and other hard surfaces. Such firms will be ideally suited for the general maintenance of parks, cemeteries, open space areas and housing and industrial landscape. There is an advantage in using one contractor on a site, who is capable of doing all that is required. Contractors of this type may be found among local, regional and national size categories although not all small local firms are equipped to deal with every aspect of this type of work.

4.2.2 Grass-cutting

Firms that offer a grass-cutting service only, can usefully be considered for verge mowing contracts and the maintenance of large open spaces. In certain circumstances they may also be used for housing landscape and cemetery work.

Grass-cutting firms are often to be found among the small local contractors, often originating from an agricultural background.

4.2.3 Forestry maintenance

Forestry contractors may be required if there are woodland areas or plantations to be maintained. The general forestry firms can be expected to be able to be conversant with all aspects of planting, establishment and maintenance work, at least up to the thinning stage, in coniferous, broadleaved and mixed plantations. Many of them will be equipped to fell mature trees in woodland areas. Forestry contractors exist throughout the whole spectrum of size categories from small local firms up to large national organizations.

4.2.4 Arboriculture

For dealing with street trees and specimen trees in parks, the services of an arboricultural contractor may be required. Such firms will employ highly trained staff and be able to undertake tree surgery, dealing with large trees as individuals rather than in woodland conditions. This is a specialist area and good firms are not numerous in some parts of the country. Again they are to be found in all three size categories.

4.2.5 Weed control

Specialist firms exist who offer a chemical weed control service on all types of hard and soft landscaped surfaces. They are to be found principally among the large national companies, sometimes being subsidiaries of the major herbicide manufacturers.

4.2.6 Aquatic work

Lakes, ponds, rivers and streams often demand the services of a contractor who specializes in this type of work. The requirement may be for dredging, weed control or the maintenance of stocks of fish and aquatic plants. Contractors with dredging equipment are likely to be found in regional and national companies but smaller firms may be able to provide the other aquatic services required.

4.2.7 Sports facilities

Firms that specialize in the construction and maintenance of outdoor sports facilities may be required. Such companies can usually offer a complete service covering all outdoor sports such as football, cricket, tennis, golf, bowls and many others. They are to be found among the regional and national companies and tend to be more numerous in the southern part of England.

4.3   SOURCES OF CONTRACTORS

Unless it is intended to use open tendering on every occasion, it will be necessary to assemble a select list of approved contractors. This is a list of firms from which selection may be made when compiling tender lists for particular contracts. The existence of such a list greatly facilitates the process of arranging tender lists as all that is necessary is to choose appropriate names from the list for the particular contract in hand.

Inclusion on a select list implies that all relevant information concerning the contractor has already been collected and this will be such as will enable the suitability of the contractor to be assessed for any particular contract. The contractor will have been required to satisfy the Authority that he or she is technically and financially eligible for inclusion on the list and all necessary enquiries as to the contractor's probity and other matters will have been made. Needless to say, the select list and all the information associated with it, is confidential and is only to be used for the purpose for which it was compiled.

Initially, the select list should comprise an appropriate number of names for immediate requirements. The subsequent maintenance of the list is an ongoing process and it should be updated and expanded as occasion arises.

Contractors for grounds maintenance may be obtained in a number of ways as follows.

4.3.1 In house

It is likely that some firms will already be known in consequence of their having been used on previous occasions by the Parks or other Departments. This should be the first line of enquiry and will usually result in a small initial list which may then be expanded from other sources. If the DLO is to be encouraged to tender for contract work, they will be included on the approved list at this stage.

4.3.2 Neighbouring Authorities

The next approach will be to contact adjoining Local Authorities with a request for information and this will produce the names of contractors who are already working in the area.

It might be thought that colleagues in 'rival' Authorities might be reluctant to disclose the names of contractors whom they employ, for fear of losing them in the future. In the writer's experience, this has never been a problem and co-operation has always been willingly given. Of course, the benefits are mutual, as information flows both ways. Where references are requested discretion should be exercised, as much of the information is of a confidential nature. References should only be given in response to a written request from a responsible officer and all such information should be treated as strictly confidential.

4.3.3 Trade lists

A number of trade and other societies produce lists of recommended contractors and these should be examined next. In order to qualify for inclusion on these lists, the companies usually have to satisfy some sort of criteria with regard to their efficiency and general reliability.

One of the most useful of these lists is that produced by BALI (British Association of Landscape Industries) and this includes a large number of firms in all parts of the country, with details of their particular specialities. The Royal Forestry Society of England Wales and Northern Ireland produce a list of forestry contractors, as does the Arboricultural Association.

4.3.4   Telephone directories

The Yellow Pages telephone directory will list the contractors in its area of circulation. They will be found in the sections headed: Landscape Gardeners, Garden Services, Turf Supplies, Turfing Services, Forestry Maintenance Services, Tree Work and Sports Ground and Playing Field Contractors. This is a good source for small local contractors.

4.3.5   Advertising

An advertisement in the local paper is likely to produce a flood of enquiries, many of which may be from contractors who prove to be unsuitable for one reason or another. Advertisements in the trade press are better, although many of the firms who respond are likely to have been picked up already, from other sources. Advertising can most usefully be employed for work of a highly specialized nature, where the number of suitable contractors is likely to be small.

It should be emphasized that these remarks refer to the general advertising for contractors to be placed on a list for possible use at some future date. They do not apply to the type of advertisement which the Local Government Act requires to be placed prior to the letting of a specific contract. In such a case, it is the contract that is being advertised, rather than the list of approved contractors. There is no reason, however, why the respondents to a contract advertisement should not also be placed on the list for future use if they so desire, provided that they appear suitable for the purpose.

4.3.6   Own approach

Once it becomes known that contract maintenance is available on a regular basis, a number of contractors will take the initiative and make their own approaches. Such contacts may be useful, although some local applicants may be unsuitable by virtue of their lack of experience or resources.

4.4 ESTABLISHING THE CREDIBILITY

Irrespective of the manner in which new contractors are introduced it will be necessary to subject them to scrutiny in order to establish their credibility before inclusion on the select list. There are four main areas which need to be examined.

4.4.1 Technical ability

First and foremost, it is necessary to ascertain that the firm has a proven track record and is capable of doing the work required in a satisfactory manner. This will entail taking up references and, whenever possible, these should be other Local Authorities, Government Departments, nationalized industries, or major land-managing services where similar work has been done. A simple questionnaire can be designed for this purpose.

Written references should not be taken at their face value but, wherever possible, the sites should be visited in order to see the standard of work produced. This is particularly relevant where private references have been given.

In addition to supplying names and addresses of persons to whom reference may be made, prospective contractors should also be asked to supply copies of Certificates of Competence held by their employees, in relation to the Control of Pesticide Regulations 1986. Failure to produce an adequate number of certificated personnel may seriously limit the nature of the work which the contractor is able to do.

4.4.2 Insurance

It is essential to ensure that all contractors have the necessary minimum amount of Public Liability insurance cover and that the Authority is indemnified against all undue claims. In this connection it will be necessary to see their insurance policy and current premium receipt or insurance certificate. The minimum amount for which they should be insured will be determined by the Finance Department, a common figure at the time of writing being £1 000 000. When examining the insurance policy attention should be paid to any exclusions, as these may inhibit the type of work which the contractor can be asked to perform.

It is sometimes considered necessary to seek a performance

bond in the case of large contracts. In many cases this is probably unnecessary where maintenance contracts are concerned, as the risk of failure and consequent financial loss is small. If there are any doubts about a contractor's financial or other ability, he or she should not be on the tender list anyway.

Only in the case of the very largest of contracts should it be necessary to consider bonding and only then if it is not possible to break it down into two or more smaller ones.

4.4.3 Payment of tax

Within the construction industry, the Finance (No 2) Act 1975 (a) requires an employer to deduct tax from all payments made to a contractor, unless the contractor is in possession of a Sub-Contractors Tax Certificate (F714C, P or I). The requirements of the Act are somewhat complicated and a certain amount of confusion has reigned in the past, as to when and where they should be applied. Generally, maintenance work is exempt, on established developments, but if any new construction is taking place on or near the maintenance area, it is likely that the contractor will need to be in possession of a tax exemption certificate. In all cases it is advisable to check the position with the local tax office before proceeding. If it is found that such a certificate is likely to be required, then it will be necessary to require the contractor to furnish proof that he or she is in possession of an up-to-date one.

If it is found that contract payments are liable to tax deductions it might be appropriate to insist on all contractors being in possession of the exemption certificate and this may be written into the Specification. In such cases it will then be necessary to check that all new contractors have the Sub-Contractors Tax Certificate and that it is valid and up to date.

4.4.4 Financial viability

It is necessary to investigate the financial position of any contractor who is seeking inclusion on the approved list. The usual procedure is to request a copy of the most recent set of Annual Accounts, a study of which should provide the necessary information.

The first consideration is to ensure that the firm has a sound financial basis which is likely to be maintained in the foreseeable future. Secondly, there should be adequate funds available for the initial financing of the proposed contract, especially if the contractor is to provide materials.

Finally, the value of any contracts offered should be related to the financial capacity of the contractor to deal with it. It is inadvisable for a firm to place all its resources, or even a major part of them, at the disposal of any one client, particularly for long-term work. A good rule of thumb in this respect is to limit the amount of work offered to about one-third to one-half of the firm's annual turnover, but different Authorities will have their own particular ideas about this. It is usual for the Finance Department to deal with these matters and to advise the Contract Manager accordingly.

4.5. TRADE INFORMATION

Contract Managers should know as much as possible about their contractors. Certain basic information is obviously required from the outset, but no opportunity should be lost to gather further information whenever the opportunity arises. The more that is known about the structure, methods of working and the long-term aims of the company, the better can the Contract Manager allocate his or her contracts. It is often useful to know how a particular firm is likely to react in a given situation and the more that is known about them the easier this becomes.

1. How long has the firm been in business and what are their long-term ambitions?
2. Do they belong to any larger group of companies?
3. Do they own any subsidiary companies?
4. Do they belong to any trade associations such as BALI; The Arboricultural Association etc?
5. Who are the Directors of the company?
6. How many full-time staff do they normally employ and of what grades?
7. What provision is made for employment of temporary labour?
8. What managerial staff are employed?
9. Who are they and what is their background?

10. Do they employ sub-contractors? If so, who are they? Do they subcontract themselves to other firms?
11. What machinery, plant and equipment do they own, or have access to?
12. Have they a nursery for supply of trees, shrubs and plants?
13. What types of work are they best able to perform?
14. Do they have any particular specialities to offer?
15. What size of contracts are they prepared to undertake?
16. Who else do they regularly work for?

The answers to these and similar questions may be obtained, over a period of time, in different ways. In some cases the contractor may be asked directly to supply certain information, e.g. by completing a questionnaire for a machinery inventory. Other questions will be answered in the course of normal conversation or from time to time as opportunity permits.

CHAPTER 5

Specifications (1)

5.1 NEED FOR A SPECIFICATION

The contract specification is a vital part of the maintenance contract, and consequently, much thought should be given to its preparation. A good specification will help to ensure that the contract runs smoothly – a bad one can be disastrous.

By 'specification' is really meant 'specification and agreement', as these two documents are usually linked together. The specification proper is concerned with the actual work to be performed under the contract and the manner in which it is to be carried out, while the agreement contains the contractual terms and general conditions of contract. These two distinct aspects of the contract are commonly produced as separate Bills of the one document which, for the sake of brevity, is usually referred to as 'the specification'. It is in this sense that the word is used here.

In an ideal world there would be no need for a written specification. All that would be required would be to tell contractors what they were expected to do, whereupon the work would be carried out and due payment made. There is no legal requirement for anything to be written down and a contract may be purely verbal, or even implied.

Unfortunately, however, the world in which we live is far from ideal and it is normal to require a fully detailed, comprehensive, written statement to be prepared, which sets out, clearly and unambiguously, the duties, responsibilities and rights of both parties to the agreement.

5.2 PURPOSE OF THE SPECIFICATION

The specification serves three main purposes as follows.

5.2.1 Preparation of tender

The specification provides a basis for contractors to prepare their tenders. The Bill of Quantities will inform contractors of the extent of the works required, thus enabling them to put a value on them. So much is obvious. What may not be realized, however, is that virtually every clause in the specification will affect the final price in some way.

Anything which restricts contractors, imposes conditions, or in any way limits their freedom of action, is liable to increase their costs or reduce their profitability and this will be reflected in their tender price. They may be required to carry a level of insurance over and above that which they would normally regard as necessary. The client might specify the use of particular types of machinery which may not be on their current inventory. Perhaps the contract requires their site foreman to provide a weekly progress report. All these things cost money and will be evaluated by contractors and included in their tenders. It follows that such restrictive clauses should be kept to a minimum and no unnecessary restraints imposed.

Other contract clauses will influence the tender price to the client's advantage. This is well illustrated in the manner of arranging contract payments. If the contract provides for regular interim payments, this will assist the contractor with his or her cash flow, thus making the financing of the contract easier. It is reasonable to expect this to be reflected in the tendered price, to the client's advantage.

5.2.2 Performance of contract

The specification directs, controls and regulates the performance of the contract.

In the operation of the contract the specification will lay down the ground rules by stating what is required, when and how it is to be done. In this it is necessary to be comprehensive and specific.

The specification should state exactly what is required, with no essential parts missed out. It is not sufficient to say 'cut the grass', if what is really meant is 'cut the grass and rake up and remove the arisings'. By and large, the contractor will do exactly what the specification says, no more and no less. The specification should contain sufficient information to leave no doubt as to what is required.

5.2.3   Protection of both parties' interests

The specification protects the interests of the parties by describing the action to be taken, and procedures to be followed, in the event of any dispute or failure on the part of either party to honour his or her contractual obligations.

It is important to remember that there are two parties involved in the contract. Although the specification will normally be prepared by the client, it should also provide for the needs of the contractor. Both parties have a right to protection and a good specification will recognize this.

Things can go wrong in various ways. The contractors might fail to do all the work required of them, or do it at the wrong time or in the wrong way. They might break the terms of their agreement by allowing their insurance cover to run out, or by employing a sub-contractor in a manner contrary to the terms of the specification. They might stop work, or even go bankrupt during the contract period.

The client might default by failing to provide facilities promised in the specification, by restricting access to the site, or otherwise impeding the contractor's work. He or she might fail to make the agreed payments at the times stated, or unreasonably attempt to deduct monies from payments due.

The specification should provide against all these contingencies, by stating what consequences may result, or what remedial actions may be taken by the injured party. In some cases the consequences of default may be written into the contract. These might provide for remedial action to be taken, as in the case of certain damage clauses ('the Contractor shall make good . . .') or perhaps entitle the injured party to claim compensation in the form of a financial adjustment.

In the event of a serious dispute which cannot be resolved by reference to the contract document, it may be desirable to submit the case to arbitration. This is made easier if the specification contains a suitably worded clause explaining the procedures to be followed in such an eventuality and describing how the arbitrator is to be chosen. It is advisable to include such provision in all but the smallest contracts.

5.3   CONTENT OF THE SPECIFICATION

In order to fulfil the purposes for which it is intended, the specification will contain appropriate clauses of the following nature:

1. Identities – basic information concerning the who, what, where and when of the contract. Definitions, abbreviations used in the documents, scope of the contract in general terms and other basic information of a general nature.
2. Description of the work – a detailed description of the work that is required, with a general indication of how it is to be done and description of the standards required.
3. Quantities – detailed breakdown of the amount or quantity of work to be carried out. The quantities given may be approximate.
4. Contractor's obligations – the special conditions with which the contractor must comply.
5. Client's obligations – that which the client undertakes to do. Includes the 'consideration', i.e. details concerning the payments and how they will be made.
6. Safeguards for the contractor – ties in with client's obligations above. May also include details of arbitration procedures in the event of a dispute.
7. Safeguards for the client – linked with contractor's obligations and usually includes procedures for dealing with unsatisfactory performance.

5.4   CHOICE OF SPECIFICATION

Having established the need for a specification and formulated the basic requirements, attention must now be directed to the choice and selection of a suitable document.

It should be stated at the outset that there is no such thing as a generally available standard document for grounds maintenance. It is doubtful if there ever will be, as individual requirements vary from one Authority to another, each having their own ideas with regard to the content and the degree of formality required. The choice is either to find an existing document which comes close to satisfying most of the requirements and amend it to suit, or to write one's own specification from the bottom up, so to speak.

There are a number of printed specifications produced by professional societies and principally intended for use by their members. These include the ICE, JCT, JCLI Agreements and others. The Property Services Agency uses a document known as GC (Works 1) and a few years ago BALI produced their 'Guide to Specifications for Grounds Maintenance'. In 1988 the Local Authority Associations published 'Competitive Tendering : Standard Core Contract Conditions and Documentation'.

In addition to these, a number of Local Authorities and New Town Development Corporations have developed documentation specifically for their own use. It is recommended that copies of these existing specifications be obtained whenever possible in order to assess their suitability, perhaps in modified form, for the purpose in hand.

5.4.1 The ICE and JCT documents

The ICE (Insititution of Civil Engineers) Conditions of Contract is a formidable document, intended mainly for works of civil engineering construction, while the JCT (Joint Contracts Tribunal for the Standard Form of Building Contract) is designed for use in the building construction industry. These documents are unsuitable for use in the context of grounds maintenance due to their highly specialized nature, the absence of matters which should be included in a grounds maintenance specification and the general style in which they are written. Many of the smaller landscape contractors do not retain solicitors or quantity surveyors on their staff and might have difficulty in appreciating some of the finer legal points contained in these documents. They are mentioned here because:

1. They are contract documents with which many Local Government Officers will be familiar, and
2. They contain some general clauses which, suitably modified, may usefully be employed in other contracts.

5.4.2 The JCLI and BALI documentation

The JCLI (Joint Council of Landscape Industries) Grounds

Maintenance Model Form of Tender and Contract Document has, as its title suggests, been specifically prepared for the type of work under consideration here. For this reason it is likely to be the most useful currently available 'model document' and contains much of value to anyone who is concerned with putting together a maintenance specification. The BALI (British Association of Landscape Industries) Guide has now been incorporated into this document.

The JCLI document is intended to be used with discrimination, by selection of the clauses to be used, with modification in some cases, and the addition of further material if required. It includes some useful notes which help one to do just this. Certainly, for the larger contracts, this would seem to be the best model upon which to base a specification, although, for smaller works, something simpler may be preferred.

5.4.3 The PSA document

The Property Services Agency for the Department of the Environment operates its contracts on a Schedule of Rates basis and uses its own GC (Works 1), supplemented with a specification for landscape work.

The GC (Works 1) is a comprehensive document, covering the Terms and Conditions of the PSA's building and civil engineering contracts. In itself, it makes no specific reference to landscape work and contains much that would be unnecessary in the context of grounds maintenance, but nevertheless contains some useful clauses of a general nature. With careful pruning and the addition of some extra material, much of it could be incorporated into a grounds maintenance contract.

5.4.4 The Local Authorities documentation

The Local Authority Associations publication and the guide which accompanies it, will be found useful reading as, being prepared by the Authorities themselves, it is most likely to reflect the needs and special requirements of Local Authorities in general. It is, however, a document written in general terms, not solely designed with grounds maintenance in mind. In particular it includes no landscape specifications.

5.4.5   Other contract documents

Specifications produced by individual Authorities vary considerably in their usefulness. Documents have been seen ranging from a mere two or three typescript pages, which said very little, to a book nearly an inch thick, which said far too much. Between these extremes are a number of specifications, some of which can be quite useful.

5.4.6   Conclusions

It will be clear from the foregoing that there is no one ideal document which can be taken off the shelf and used as it stands, without alteration or amendment, for Local Authority grounds maintenance. For the very large or long-term contracts, it is worth considering the adaptation of existing specifications and for this purpose the JCLI and PSA documents will be found most useful.

In some cases, however, it may be considered more appropriate to use a shorter, simpler type of specification and this will need to be produced in house. Such a document can be assembled without too much difficulty by following the methods outlined in the following chapter.

CHAPTER 6

Specifications (2)

6.1 AUTHORSHIP

If the Contract Specification is to be prepared in house the first consideration will be – who is to write it?

As the Specification is a legal document it might at first be thought that it should be prepared by the legal department. In the case of small maintenance contracts, however, this is not necessarily a good idea, for at least two reasons.

First, comes the problem of legal language. A contract produced by lawyers may be overburdened with legal terminology, to the extent that it becomes necessary to employ a solicitor to interpret it. Small contractors can be intimidated by legal phraseology and it is important that this be kept to a minimum. The aim should be to express everything in simple straightforward terms, consistent with the need for precision in the choice of words. Legal phrases should only be used where they are absolutely necessary – a good Specification is a readable Specification.

Secondly, the legal department is unlikely to be aware of the technical input required so that it will be necessary to prepare a technical Specification at least, as well as to brief them regarding the nature of a number of general clauses which will be required. By the time this has been done one might as well go one stage further and write the Specification oneself.

The Quantity Surveyor is the next person to be considered as a possible writer of the Specification. On the face of it, this seems to be an ideal choice, as he or she will be familiar with similar types of documents and probably have sufficient knowledge of horticultural matters to interpret the draft Specifications appropriately. The problem here is that the Quantity Surveyor is generally more familiar with construction contracts which, by their nature, are tightly specified and very precise, particularly with regard to the quantitative elements of the Specification.

A maintenance contract generally needs to be much more flexible than a construction contract. Quantities are approximate and variable and many maintenance operations are subject to seasonal, weather and growing conditions. Consequently, the maintenance Specification should be sufficiently open-ended to allow for this and generally will lack the precision of the average landscape construction Specification. If the Quantity Surveyor is prepared to relax his or her usual standards and take a more flexible approach, with less emphasis on the quantitative elements, the resulting Specification is likely to be perfectly acceptable, but not all Quantity Surveyors may be prepared to do this.

The best person to write the Specification will be the one who is going to use it – the Parks Manager, or Contract Manager, as the case might be. Provided that this officer is familiar in general terms with contract documentation, he or she should be able to produce a Specification which embodies all that is required, written in a practical manner which will appeal to the average small contractor.

6.2 STRUCTURE AND CONTENT

Before starting, it will be advisable to obtain copies of as many similar documents as possible and study them closely, in order to find the best possible way to express the various ideas which must be incorporated. It is usual to present the information in the form of separate Bills.

6.2.1 Bill No. 1

Bill No. 1 will be the Preliminaries, or Preamble, containing general information concerning the scope of the contract, essential dates and names, definitions and abbreviations used in the document.

6.2.2 Bill No. 2

Bill No. 2 will comprise the general terms and conditions of the contract. It will refer to such matters as standards of work, provision of labour, tools, machinery and materials and provision for water supply and tipping facilities. It will contain damage clauses and will detail the insurance, tax and any other requirements with which the contractor must comply. Methods of payment will be described, including reference to retention money if applicable. Retention of payments due is not normally considered necessary in the case of maintenance contracts, provided that the client has the right to withhold part or all of an interim payment if the works are unsatisfactory or not up to date. Exception might be made in the case of herbicide application, or if replanting is required, when part of the payment might be retained until such time as the operation has been seen to have been effective.

Any legislation with which the contractor should comply will be noted in this Bill.

6.2.3   Bill No. 3

Bill No. 3 will be the Specification itself, i.e. a detailed description of the work that is to be performed. It will state the frequency of operations and, where applicable, when they should be carried out. Care must be taken to include everything that the contractor will be expected to do, as anything that is not specifically mentioned in the Specification will be regarded as not part of the contract. Such items, if subsequently ordered, will then become liable to extra payment over and above the contract price.

The client is entitled to specify how he or she wants the work to be done but it is unwise to place unnecessary restrictions on the contractor in this respect. To do so might inhibit some firms from tendering, result in higher tenders, or both. By way of example, it is better to refer to 'motor triple mower' rather than to name any individual make of equipment, unless there is a particular reason for requiring the use of a specific machine.

6.2.4   Bill No. 4 (the Bill of Quantities)

Bill No. 4 (the Bill of Quantities) will quantify the work required although, as previously stated, such quantities will be approximate ones, correct at the time of compilation. The Bill will list such items as grass areas, possibly arranged in categories, shrub bed areas, areas and types of bedding and other planted beds, number of trees, possibly by size categories – in short anything and everything that is included in the contract, that is capable of being counted or measured, will be listed. The contractors will use this information when compiling their tender so it is important that it be complete and as accurate as circumstances permit. If the quantites are provided for guidance only, the information is best presented in the form of a 'Landscape Schedule'. If, however, it is intended that the contractors should affix their prices to the quantities, as part of their tender, then the Bill of Quantities is the usual form.

6.2.5 Bill No. 5

Bill No. 5 may be a Schedule of Rates. This is optional but it may be useful to obtain the contractor's unit rates for individual, specified items of work, in order to facilitate the pricing of variations and any additional work which may be required in connection with the contract.

Finally, certain items may usefully be included in the form of appendices to the Specification. These may include location maps, diagrams and supplementary information.

6.3 WRITING THE SPECIFICATION

When writing the Specification it is advisable to take each Bill separately and start by listing the clauses likely to be required in each one. The wording of each individual clause may be determined by reference to what others have said on a similar subject in any other documents which may be to hand. Choose the form which best expresses the meaning which it is desired to impart and adjust the actual wording according to specific requirements. The result should be clear and concise and unambiguous. Use simple language where possible with the minimum amount of legal phraseology. Do not be afraid to use legal language, however, where it appears necessary in order to convey the precise shade of meaning, but beware of using legal expressions if their true meaning is not fully understood.

Be careful to distinguish between words such as 'may' 'will' and 'shall'. If in doubt, reference to works such as Gower's *Complete Plain Words*, or *Modern English Usage* by Fowler, may be found useful.

Avoid repetition – it is easy to fall into the trap of repeating something which has already been covered by a previous clause. Even more importantly, beware of contradiction. It is patently easy to say something which is contradictory to what has been said in another part of the Specification. Careful checking, after the whole of the document has been drafted, should uncover any errors of this nature.

Care must also be taken to ensure that the Specification is free from all reference to 'non-commercial matters'. Part 2 of The Local Government Act prohibits such references in connection with the inclusion of a contractor on an approved list and in tendering procedures for a grounds maintenance contract.

Non-commercial matters are defined as:

1. The terms and conditions of employment by a contractor of their workers
2. The terms of employment of sub-contractors
3. Involvement by the contractor with irrelevant fields of government policy
4. The conduct of a contractor or their workforce with regard to industrial disputes
5. The territorial interests of contractors
6. The political interests of contractors
7. Any financial support given or withheld by a contractor to any institution
8. The use or non-use of technical or professional support provided by the Authority

Thus it would be wrong, for instance, for an Authority to debar an otherwise eligible contractor from an approved list, on the grounds that the firm has interests in South Africa. Equally, it is not permitted to specify minimum rates of pay which a contractor's employees must receive.

The Authority has a duty to ensure that these non-commercial matters play no part in the arranging of a grounds maintenance contract.

After all the clauses of a particular Bill have been written, they should be assembled in some sort of logical order. If word processing facilities are available it will be found useful to put the Specification on to disc as soon as the first draft has been prepared. It will probably be necessary to revise and rewrite parts of the document several times before a satisfactory final result is obtained and it is comparatively easy to alter and to move things around on the screen.

6.4 THE COMPLETED DOCUMENT

Once the writing of the Specification has been completed and has received its final checks for errors, a copy should be submitted to the Authority's legal representatives with a request that they examine it for legal inconsistencies or omissions. It is to be hoped that there will be none, but they may wish to suggest one or two minor alterations which will improve the legal credibility of the document. If so, their advice should be taken, provided that there is no alteration to the underlying meaning of the text as originally designed. The document, then in its final form, may be submitted for printing and the Specification will then be available for contract use.

The Milton Keynes Specification, a copy of which will be found at the end of this book, is an example of a maintenance Specification which has been written in the manner described above.

6.5 THE MASTER DOCUMENT

It will be found useful to prepare a 'master copy' of the completed document so that this can be used to prepare Specifications for other contracts where similar conditions apply. This master document is prepared by omitting all dates, site names and quantities, but leaving appropriate spaces for their insertion. It is then a simple matter to prepare a Specification for any particular contract site by insertion of the specific details in a copy of the master document.

6.6 REVISION OF THE SPECIFICATION

Before the start of each contract term it is advisable to consider the need for revisions of the standard Specification and, if necessary, to make whatever modifications are required, before issuing new contracts. Such modifications may be necessary to take account of changing legislation or to take advantage of new techniques and improved equipment and materials.

It is sometimes necessary to modify certain clauses, or to delete or introduce new ones, in the light of previous experience. We should be aware of the danger of complacency; with hindsight it is often possible to rewrite something or to express it in a better way than that which was considered appropriate at an earlier date. That is not to say that there was necessarily anything wrong with the Specification as previously written. It might have been perfectly adequate at the time it was written, but with experience and to take account of changing circumstances and conditions, it is wise to review it from time to time.

Of course, it is not possible to alter any of the contract terms during the currency of the contract, we have to live with what we have got, although if the relationship between contractor and client is as it should be, it is sometimes possible to agree minor changes on an informal basis. The good old-fashioned principle of 'swings and roundabouts' is appropriate here, but this obviously depends on the extent of the goodwill which exists between the two parties to the contract and certainly cannot be enforced by any legal means unless both parties are in full agreement.

CHAPTER 7

Estimates

7.1 THE CONCEPT OF AN ESTIMATE

At some stage in the preparation of the contract it will be necessary to produce an estimate. This is a subject about which much confusion exists and it is necessary to define exactly what is meant by the term and to evolve a satisfactory method of calculation.

First, let it be said that there is no such thing as a 'correct' estimate, but that some estimates are more acceptable than others. One of the characteristics of the maintenance contract is the wide divergence of the tenders submitted for any one contract. This matter is discussed at greater length in a later chapter but is mentioned here in view of its effect on the credibility of the estimate.

It is generally accepted that an estimate should be prepared, prior to tendering, and that the tenders, when received, should approximate to the estimate. However, if the tenders are wide ranging only one or two may be anywhere near the estimate. It is even possible that none of them may be sufficiently close to the estimate to be regarded as acceptable. In these circumstances, how are we to know whether it is the estimate that is at fault or the tenders, and if the latter, which ones?

7.2 REASONS FOR THE ESTIMATE

In spite of these difficulties, a contract estimate should normally be prepared for the following reasons:

1. It is necessary to have some idea of the size of the contract so that priority can be given to the larger and most important ones. We might wish to divide our contracts into small,

medium and large categories and this can only be done by putting values on them.

2. The value of the contract will be a major factor in selecting contractors for the tender list, as it will be necessary to ensure that the selected contractors are matched to the contract, in terms of size and available resources.

3. The estimate may be used as a yardstick against which the client (and in particular a lay committee) may measure the tender results.

7.3   DEFINING THE ESTIMATE

Before attempting to define and describe the estimate, it would be well to get rid of one or two misconceptions.

In the first place, the estimate is not intended to equate exactly with the eventual contract price. This will not be known until after the contract has been awarded and any attempt to predict it is likely to be unsuccessful.

Secondly, the estimate is not intended to represent the 'value' of the contract, whatever that might mean. 'Value' and 'worth' are words which mean different things to different people. Clients would like to think that their contracts would be executed for something less than their actual 'value'. Conversely, they would not expect to have to pay more than they consider them to be 'worth'.

Thirdly, the estimate is not the DLO price, i.e. the cost that would be incurred if we were to carry out the work with our own staff. In many cases, this would be a sure-fire way of ensuring that all our contracts were let at below estimate prices, but the value of such 'estimates' would be minimal.

For practical purposes it is suggested that the contract estimate may be loosely defined as : a value attached to a contract, prepared in advance of tendering, and approximating to the average of the tenders received. In other words, we are not seeking to predict the value of the lowest tender, but the average of all the tenders submitted (known as the tender average).

It follows from the above definition that the estimate can never be accurately calculated, as the precise values of the tenders are not known at the time it is prepared. In spite of this, methods exist for preparation of estimates which are within acceptable limits. The difference between the estimate and the tender average is known as the error in the estimate and this should be kept within reasonable bounds. We shall return to a discussion of these matters, as well as attempting a more rigorous definition of the estimate, after describing how the estimate is prepared.

7.4 PREPARATION OF THE PROVISIONAL ESTIMATE

The contract estimate is prepared in three stages and the first of these involves calculation of a provisional estimate. This is compiled from site data and known costs and can be prepared as soon as the landscape schedule becomes available.

There are a number of ways in which a provisional estimate can be prepared and no one method is likely to produce an ideal result. The recommended procedure, therefore, is to produce a number of estimates by different methods and to take an average of these. By so doing, some of the errors inherent in each one may be cancelled out and the maximum error present, reduced.

Of the following methods, only the first three will be available at the commencement of the first contract year. The others cannot be implemented until the relevant data has been collected as a result of previous tendering. Consequently, the estimates are likely to improve with time, as the information obtained as the result of the initial round of tendering is fed back into the system, to provide a wider basis for the preparation of future estimates.

7.4.1 The DLO method

This is calculated from known operational costs of the Direct Labour Organization. Care must be taken to include only those items which are included in the contract, adjusted if necessary to conform to the contract specification. If the contract requires the contractor to supply materials, these should be priced to include handling and administrative charges and delivery to site. Do not forget to include operational costs of machinery and plant, including fuel. Include Departmental overheads but not the general overhead of your Authority. Allow for inflation and include a minimum of 5% for profit.

7.4.2 Spon's estimate

Using the latest edition of *Spon's Landscape and External Works Price Book*, calculate the value of the contract quantities on the basis of the prices listed. Any items not priced in *Spon's* should be assessed in terms of the number of working-hours likely to be involved and then multiplied by the appropriate hourly rate. Add for materials if required, and adjust for inflation. A deduction of 5%–20% may be made, according to the size of the contract, in recognition of the large quantities involved.

7.4.3 Rule of thumb

This method is not as precise as the two previous ones but should not be neglected on that account. The method is based more on practical experience of site maintenance than on any sophisticated calculations or considerations of individual unit prices. It is not even necessary to be aware of the landscape quantities in order to practise this method of estimating.

Quite simply, the contract site is walked by an experienced grounds operative or supervisor, who assesses the amount of work to be done in terms of man-hours per unit for each particular operation. These figures are then multiplied by the number of units needed during the year and the total hours so obtained are applied to a known hourly rate to produce the annual labour cost. Likewise, using his or her experience, the assessor will determine the number and types of machine needed and the machine hours for the year. This enables the machinery costs to be calculated. The cost of materials is then added and the figures totalled up. After adding an appropriate percentage for overheads and profit, the resultant figure becomes the rule of thumb estimate. This method does not appear to be very scientific but it is remarkable how accurate it may prove to be in practice, provided that the assessor is well versed in the practical operations concerned. This method is probably the one most commonly employed by the small contractor.

7.4.4 Previous contract

This method can be used when the site has been the subject of a previous contract. Starting with the previous contract price, make appropriate adjustments as follows:

1. Area: Is this the same as before? Have the quantities been increased or decreased?
2. Timespan: Is this the same or has the contract period been lengthened or decreased?
3. Materials: Any variation in the materials required compared with the previous contract?
4. Specification: Any major alterations which are liable to affect the price?
5. Inflation: Allow for the number of years since the contract was last tendered.
6. State of the market: Is the competition likely to be greater or less than on the previous occasion?

7.4.5 Alternative contract

Similar to the above but based on the contract price of another similar contract. The previous contract price is adjusted as in the method described above, paying particular attention to (a) the quantities and (b) the materials.

7.4.6 Schedule of rates

This involves building up an estimate from the Bill of Quantities using contractor's unit rates. These rates will have been obtained incidentally in the course of normal business relations with existing contractors, or purposefully from the Schedules of Rates submitted annually by local firms (Chapter 10). Each itemized quantity should be multiplied by the average of the available rates and the number of occasions in the year that it is required. An allowance should be made for day work items and the result totalled. A reduction of 5%–20% is made for large quantities. After adjusting for inflation, the value of materials is added to produce a final figure.

It will not always be possible to utilize all these different methods but the aim should be to produce as many as the available data will permit. The provisional estimate may then be calculated by taking the average (median) value.

The median is to be preferred to the mean in this case, as it will generally be found that one of the estimates will be exceptionally high, or low, compared with the others and this would give a distorted average were the mean value to be calculated.

To calculate the median, arrange the estimates in size order and simply select the middle value.

Example

Suppose that: estimate A = £25 300
estimate B = £30 500
estimate C = £18 000

Placing these in size order gives: 18 000
25 300
30 500

when it may be seen that the central value is 25 300.
Thus E_1 = £25 300
where E_1 = Provisional Estimate

If the number of estimates is an even number the median is found by taking the mean of the two central values.

Example

Where A = £25 300
B = £30 500
C = £18 000
D = £26 800

Placing in order gives 18 000
25 300
26 800
30 500

Here, the two central values are 25 300 and 26 800, so the median value is:

$$\frac{25\ 300\ +\ 26\ 800}{2} = 26\ 050$$

giving E_1 = £26 050

Having calculated the provisional estimate, this may now be used as an approximate measure of the contract's size, enabling an appropriate list of contractors to be assembled for tender purposes. Once this has been done, the estimate can be further refined by weighting, as follows.

7.5 PREPARATION OF THE WEIGHTED ESTIMATE

If the final estimate is to represent the average of the actual tenders submitted, the tender list must influence, in some way, the size of the estimate. This is achieved by weighting the provisional estimate according to the contractors selected to tender for it.

Experience will soon reveal those contractors who can be relied upon to submit the lowest tenders in the majority of cases. Likewise, firms who regularly tender in fourth or fifth place will soon be identified. Between the two extremes come the majority of tenderers whose tender performance is less predictable. What is required is some method of quantifying each firm's average tender performance, so that a value may be attached to each one. These values may then be used to weight the provisional estimate in the light of the tender list. If sufficient statistical data is available, a somewhat sophisticated method of calculating this is by means of the Contractor's Tender Factor.

The Contractor's Tender Factor (CTF) may be calculated from the results of previous tendering as follows:

1. Consider the results of all contracts over the previous two-year period.
2. For each contractor involved, list the contracts for which he or she has submitted valid tenders.
3. In each case, divide the tender by the provisional estimate for that contract. This will give a figure which is usually between 0.500 and 1.500, and represents that contract's Tender Factor in respect of one particular contract, i.e.

$$F = \frac{T}{E_1}$$

where F = the CTF
        T = the tender
        E_1 = the provisional estimate

4. Repeat for each contract in which that contractor has been involved during the period. Add these factors together and divide by their number to produce an average. This will be the Contractor's Tender Factor for that particular year.

The CTF will need to be recalculated each year, using the preceding two years results, in order to keep it up to date. If there are to be several opportunities given to a contractor during the current year, the CTF may be calculated as a moving factor by adding in the results of each tender as soon as it becomes known. A contractor who has no previous tender history is given the neutral factor of 1.000.

Having calculated the CTF for each contractor on the tender list the weighted estimate is obtained by the following method:

1. Examine the tender list and select the three contractors with the lowest CTFs.
2. Multiply the sum of those factors by the provisional estimate and divide the result by 3. This will produce the weighted estimate for that contract, i.e.

$$E_2 = \frac{E_1(F_1 + F_2 + F_3)}{3}$$

where E_2 = the weighted estimate
   E_1 = the provisional estimate
and F_1, F_2, F_3 = the CTFs for the three contractors selected

In cases where it is neither practical nor desirable to calculate the Contractor's Tender Factor, a judgement must be taken as to which firms are considered likely to provide the lowest tenders. As with all statistical methods, the calculation of the CTF is only likely to be worth while if sufficient data is available to support it.

7.6   PREPARATION OF THE FINAL ESTIMATE

The weighted estimate should be more accurate than the provisional estimate as it takes into account the tender performance of the contractors concerned. In practice, however, this may not always be the case. The calculations being based on past form, the result will only be true if all the contractors continue to tender true to form. As this seldom happens, one final adjustment must be made.

We have no way of predicting how any deviations from past form will be manifest, so in order to reduce possible errors to a minimum, we take the average of the provisional and weighted estimates and this becomes the final estimate, i.e.

$$E_3 = \frac{E_1 + E_2}{2}$$

where
E_1 = the provisional estimate
E_2 = the weighted estimate
E_3 = the final estimate

The final estimate will usually be found to be sufficiently close to the average tender to satisfy most normal requirements.

7.7 THE ERROR PERCENTAGE

It has previously been stated that the estimate should approximate to the tender average. It is unlikely that these two figures will ever be exactly the same and their difference is known as the error in the estimate (E_e). This is conveniently expressed as a percentage, which is calculated by

$$E_e = \frac{E_3 - T_{ave}}{T_{ave}} \times 100$$

where
E_e = the error percentage
E_3 = the final estimate
T_{ave} = the tender average

The error percentage may be positive or negative. This leads on to the concept of acceptable error.

7.8 THE ACCEPTABLE ERROR

Since it is unlikely that the error in the estimate will ever be zero, small errors must be accepted. Estimates with large errors, however, would be of little value. What do we mean by 'small' and 'large' in this context? It has been found in practice that 15% is a reasonable figure (albeit a somewhat arbitrary one) to aim at, so that an acceptable error may be defined as an error that falls within ±15% of the tender average. We are now in a position to redefine our estimate in terms of an 'acceptable' estimate.

7.9   THE ACCEPTABLE ESTIMATE

An acceptable estimate is a value prepared in advance of tendering, which approximates to the tender average, with an error of not more than ±15%. Alternatively, if a shorter version is preferred: 'an acceptable estimate is one with acceptable error'.

7.10   WORKED EXAMPLE

The following worked example may help to make clear some of the matters discussed in the preceding pages.

It is assumed that a Grounds Maintenance Contract is to go out to tender. The quantities have been identified and a Bill of Quantities prepared. The estimate is then prepared as follows:

7.10.1   Provisional Estimate (E_1)

Working from the B of Q, separate estimates are prepared using the first three methods described in this chapter. This results in:

DLO Estimate	£46 600
Spon's Estimate	£54 750
Rule of Thumb Estimate	£44 310

so that the **Provisional Estimate = £46 600** = E_1

7.10.2   Weighted Estimate (E_2)

Having selected five contractors for the tender list we examine their previous tendering history over the last two years and calculate the Contractor's Tender Factor for each, if this has not already been prepared in anticipation. The Tender list is as follows:

$$
\begin{array}{lll}
\text{Contractor } A & \text{CTF} = 1.231 \\
\text{Contractor } B & \text{CTF} = 0.774 \\
\text{Contractor } C & \text{CTF} = 1.090 \\
\text{Contractor } D & \text{CTF} = 1.000 \\
\text{Contractor } E & \text{CTF} = 0.989
\end{array}
$$

Selecting the three lowest CTFs gives:

$$
\begin{array}{lll}
B & 0.774 & = F_1 \\
E & 0.989 & = F_2 \\
D & 1.000 & = F_3
\end{array}
$$

Thus
$$
E_2 = \frac{E_1(F_1 + F_2 + F_3)}{3}
$$

$$
= \frac{46\,600(0.774 + 0.989 + 1.000)}{3}
$$

$$
= \frac{46\,600 \times 2.763}{3}
$$

$$
= 42\,918.60
$$

This is rounded to   42 920

Therefore the **Weighted Estimate** = **£42 920** = E_2

7.10.3 Final Estimate (E_3)

From the above data: $E_3 = \dfrac{E_1 + E_2}{2}$

$$
= \frac{46\,600 + 42\,920}{2}
$$

$$
= 44\,760
$$

Thus, the **Final Estimate** = **£44 760** = E_3

7.10.4 Tender Average (T_{ave})

Tenders were eventually received for this contract as follows:

Tender *A*	£68 250
Tender *B*	£36 700
Tender *C*	£43 560
Tender *D*	£46 250
Tender *E*	£42 785

The Tender Average is therefore:

$$T_{ave} = \frac{T_1 + T_2 + T_3 + T_4 + T_5}{5}$$

$$= \frac{68\ 250 + 36\ 700 + 43\ 560 + 46\ 250 + 42\ 785}{5}$$

$$= 47\ 509$$

i.e. **The Tender Average = £47 509** = T_{ave}

7.10.5 Error Percentage (E_e)

$$E_e = \frac{E_3 - T_{ave}}{T_{ave}} \times 100$$

$$= \frac{44\ 760 - 47\ 509}{47\ 509} \times 100$$

$$= -\frac{2749}{47\ 509} \times 100$$

$$= -5.79$$

Thus the **Error Percentage = 5.80%** = E_e

CHAPTER 8

Tenders and tendering

It is normal to let contracts by competitive tender. This is not the only way, it may not even be the best way, but for reasons of probity and public accountability, it is the way that public authorities are expected to do it.

Ideally, competitive tendering demands that the tenders should all be truly comparable, so that the eventual selection can be made on the basis of the price alone. For this reason, qualified tenders may not normally be acceptable. It is important that no tenderer shall be privy to information not also available to his or her competitors. This is achieved by sending out an identical package containing full and complete information to all the tenderers at the same time. The closing date should be strictly adhered to.

8.1 THE TENDER LIST

8.1.1 Selection from an approved list

The contractors who are to be invited to tender for the contract should be chosen with care. The aim should be to match suitable firms to particular contracts. This should be done having regard to their size, type and degree of expertise available, their resources in terms of labour and equipment and their financial status. In general, the small contracts will be offered to small firms and the large ones to the bigger companies – horses for courses.

Other factors may be taken into consideration, such as geographical distribution and known existing work-loads. It is assumed that a list will be available of 'approved' contractors from which selection may be made. Such vital matters as insurance cover, financial viability etc., will have been checked out well in advance of the tendering season.

It is usual to select five appropriate contractors to tender for each contract. This is not an arbitrary number, but is derived as follows.

First of all, the aim is to obtain at least three valid tenders. If we have only one tender, this tells us very little. We have no means of knowing whether it is a realistic figure, excessively high, or excessively low. There is no contest and our only choice is to take it or leave it.

If there are two tenders, this is better, but if there is much variation between them we still do not know which is the more realistic. Is the lower one too low or the higher one too high?

With three tenders we can start to take averages. It is likely that two of them will be reasonably close together although the third may be way out, either above or below. Statistically, four is better and five is better still.

In order to obtain three tenders we obviously need at least three contractors on the tender list, but it is possible that one of them may not respond. By offering to five we are likely to get three or more tenders submitted. It would be unusual to get less than three from this number.

Any number over five is usually unnecessary and only involves us and our contractors in needless expense. It should be realized that it costs an Authority money to send out tender documentation and to process the results. From the contractor's point of view, it costs money to respond to a tender invitation and for each contract, only one of the tenderers is going to receive any recompense for their labours. It seems unfair to expect an unnecessarily large number of companies to expend the time, money and effort, in every case. In the long term, the effect of such a policy would be to increase the cost of contracts generally, as there is no other way that the contractors could recover these expenses. The important thing, of course, is to share out the opportunities in such a way that, over the total tender period, all eligible contractors get opportunities to tender for their fair share of the available contracts.

A somewhat sophisticated method of compiling a tender list involves the use of the contractor's tender factor as described in a previous chapter. First identify and list all those contractors who might be considered appropriate for a particular contract by virtue of their size, type, known resources, availability and other factors. To each one attach his current CTF.

Suppose we have a list of nine firms from which we require to select five for a tender list. Arrange the list in size order of their CTFs. We might have something like the following:

$$\text{Contractor } A : 0.612$$
$$B : 0.876$$
$$C : 0.990$$
$$D : 1.005$$
$$E : 1.035$$
$$F : 1.150$$
$$G : 1.241$$
$$H : 2.300$$
$$I : 4.710$$

The lowest tenders are likely to be submitted by the contractors with the lowest CTFs. Therefore our first choice will be A, B, C, D and E. We would like the tenders to be fairly close together, i.e. the difference between the lowest and the highest should not be excessive. At this stage, the range will be indicated by the range of the CTFs and in the above example this will be:

$$E - A = 1.035 - 0.612 = 0.423$$

which seems reasonable. Inspection of the above table, however, reveals that A is particularly low, compared with the others. This will become more apparent if the values are plotted on a graph (see Figure 8.1(a). This provides an early warning that we might get an inordinately low tender for this contract.

Now consider the next group – B C D E and F. The range is:

$$F - B = 1.150 - 0.876 = 0.274$$

This looks much better with a range which should produce much closer tendering Fig. 8.1(b). In these circumstances the suggested tender list would be B, C, D, E and F. The contractors not chosen in this instance would of course be included in subsequent lists, when a similar procedure might be applied.

8.1.2 Selection by advertisement

If an Authority has placed an advertisement in a local paper in accordance with the requirements of The Local Government Act there will likely be a number of applications from contractors

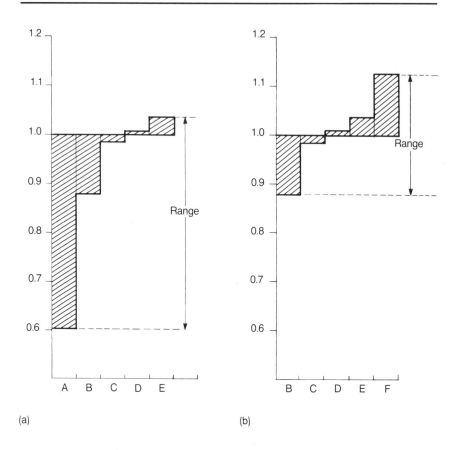

Figure 8.1 Range of tenders

who wish to be considered for the work. The procedure then is:

1. If the DLO has notified its wish to bid for the work it will be invited to do so.
2. If not more than three private contractors have notified their intention, all will be invited.
3. If more than three private contractors have applied, at least three will be invited to tender and more than three if the Authority so decides. In this event, the Authority may wish to select three (or more) from the total number of applicants and much of the foregoing section will then apply.
4. If one or more approved authorities have applied, the Authority may or may not accept them, as it wishes.

If contractors have been selected on to a tender list who have not previously been included on an approved list, immediate steps should then be taken to assess their suitability and elegibility for the work. It would be embarrassing and time wasting to allow a contractor to submit the lowest tender for a contract only to find that they were ineligible for one reason or another.

8.2 INTENTION TO TENDER (ITT)

Having prepared a provisional tender list, with all but the smallest contracts it is recommended that each of the selected contractors be invited to confirm their intention to submit a tender. In the majority of cases, of course, the answer will be in the affirmative, but occasionally a contractor may decline the opportunity if he feels that he is not likely to have the resources available to handle the contract, or for some other reason. In this event, there will be an opportunity to substitute another tenderer in his place, thus maximizing the number of valid tenders likely to be received.

The Intention to Tender Form is discussed further in Chapter 11.

8.3 THE TENDER PACKAGE

On return of the ITTs no time should be lost in preparing the tender packages and sending these out to the final list of tenderers. The package will include the following:

1. Specification(s)
2. Drawings
3. Instructions for Tendering
4. Tender Forms
5. Return envelope
6. Non-tender Form
7. Supplementary Schedules
8. Letter of invitation

One of each item should be sent, with the exception of the Tender Form and, possibly, the Specification. Two Tender Forms will be required in order that the contractor may retain a copy of his tender and this will also apply to the Specification if it contains a Bill of Quantities or Schedules of Rates which requires pricing. If not, however, a single copy will suffice for tendering purposes. At a later stage, the successful tenderer may be provided with additional copies of the Specification and drawings for contract use.

Most of the items listed above are self-explanatory and some of them are further described in Chapter 11. The Non-tender Form deserves a mention here, however, as its use may not be familiar to all.

8.4   NON-TENDER FORM

Even though the tenderers may have expressed their original intention to tender for a contract it sometimes happens that not all, in fact, do so. Contractors may announce their willingness to tender in good faith but, during the time which elapses before receiving the tender documents, their situation may have changed. They may have secured other work in the interim, confirmation of which was not to hand at the earlier date. In these circumstances they may not, after all, have the resources to take on anything else and thus be forced to decline the invitation.

Occasionally, a firm may feel obliged to tender, having expressed their prior intention, and will submit an inflated offer, expecting not to be successful, rather than not submit a tender at all. This practice is of no good to anyone but does, regrettably, occur.

In order to obviate this possibility a form may be included in the tender package, for return only if the contractor wishes not to submit a tender. An example of a suitable form for this purpose will be found in Chapter 11.

It should be made clear that the return of a Non-tender Form, with a valid reason for declining, within the tender period, will not prejudice the contractor's chances on a future occasion. This, although a nuisance, is far better than receiving an obviously inflated tender or perhaps no response at all, which latter, if repeated, might lead to the removal of the contractor's name from the approved list.

The tender packages should all be despatched at the same time, preferably by first class post. The additional cost is justified in the interests of expediency and the greater attention which they can be expected to receive in the hands of the postal authorities. The person or persons responsible for arranging for the receipt of tenders should be notified as soon as they have been despatched and advised of the closing date and time, in order that they can prepare for the eventual return of the tenders.

8.5 RECEIPT OF TENDERS

The tenders should be opened as soon as possible after the closing date. They should be opened in the presence of a senior officer, in front of witnesses. The names of the tenderers and the amounts tendered will be recorded before handing them over for processing. Late tenders should not be accepted under any circumstances, with the possible exception of those which may have been delayed by postal strikes or other circumstances outside the control of the sender. In such cases it may be permissible to accept them, provided that some proof that they were posted in ample time is available and that the other tenders have not already been opened.

The tenders should all be validated before any consideration is given to selection of the winning contractor. First, check that the tender form has been correctly and completely filled in with all necessary signatures and dates, including witnesses. Check the tender price and ensure that the written price agrees with the amount in figures. Check the arithmetic if applicable. If the tender includes any priced Bills or Schedules of Rates, ensure that these are completed correctly, with correct totals carried forward and that the total amount agrees with the price as stated on the tender form.

Examine all the documents returned and ensure that there are no qualifications and that no unauthorized amendments have been made.

Assuming that all is in order, the next step is to examine the amounts tendered and to select the winning tender. This will normally be the lowest tender submitted. Compare this figure with the tender estimate. It is to be hoped that the lowest tender will be close to the estimate, ideally just below it. This tender can then be recommended for acceptance and the contract awarded to the firm which has submitted it.

Occasionally, there are problems at this stage. Things do not always work out as expected. Some of the situations which might arise are as follows.

8.5.1   Lowest tender higher than estimate

Where the lowest tender is substantially higher than the estimate, check the estimate. If five contractors have tendered substantially higher than the estimate there must be some reason for it. In the end we must decide whether the lowest tender can be accepted, in spite of the estimate. If not, then it might be possible to negotiate a lower price with the lowest tenderer. Failing this, the contract must be aborted and consideration given to going out to tender again on a different basis. Possibly, the contract can be split into two smaller ones, or conversely, made larger by the addition of extra work. It is usually best to accept the lowest tender, however, as we are probably unlikely to do any better the second time around and we may finish up paying even more.

8.5.2   Lowest tender lower than estimate

Where the lowest tender is substantially lower than the estimate it is necessary to examine the second and other tenders. Sometimes we may get a tender which appears unrealistic while the second tender is close to the estimate. If the lowest tender is such that we do not believe that the contractor can carry out the work to the required standard, at his or her stated price, we should inform them of the situation and invite them to check their tender. If they subsequently find that their tender is deficient in some respect they may be allowed to withdraw it, thus leaving the way clear for consideration to be given to the next tender in order.

On the other hand, if the contractor finds that there is no mistake, and is prepared to stand by the tender, then we have little option but to accept, in spite of our misgivings.

If it is found that the second tender is also low, compared with the estimate, then it is necessary to check the estimate. In any case, there is little point in inviting the lowest tenderer to withdraw if the second one also appears unrealistic. In these circumstances the lowest tender should be accepted but the contractor should be apprised of the situation and given the opportunity to check his or her figures before the contract is finalized.

8.5.3 Identical tenders submitted

Two identical tenders are submitted in the lowest tender position. This is very rare but can occasionally happen. It may be possible to decide between them on the basis of some other financial factor such as the Schedule of Rates, if the tender includes one. Failing this, the two contractors should be apprised of the situation and asked if they would be prepared to resubmit after modifying their tenders. If this fails to produce a satisfactory result the contract should be aborted and re-tendered as in Section 8.5.1 above.

8.6 NOTIFICATION OF RESULTS

Having decided to which tenderer the contract should be awarded, all the tenderers should be notified without delay. Opinions differ as to how much information should be divulged at this stage. Confidentiality demands that the tenders submitted by particular firms should not be disclosed to others. On the other hand, losing contractors will want to know that they lost fairly and by how much, so that they may have the opportunity to improve their performance on another occasion.

It is suggested that, at the least, each tenderer should eventually be informed of the values of all tenders received. This will help to instil confidence and provide a valuable piece of market information which will be of future benefit.

The building industry has developed its own 'NJCC Code of Procedure for Single Stage Selective Tendering' and this may be usefully studied in connection with the matters discussed in this chapter. A copy of the Code is usefully included as an appendix in *Spon's Landscape Contract Manual*.

CHAPTER 9

Supervision

9.1 THE IMPORTANCE OF SUPERVISION

The importance of adequate supervision of the maintenance contract cannot be over-emphasized. Any contract will not run itself, however, much as we might like to think so and it is up to the Employer to provide the necessary back-up in this respect.

Please note that we are talking here of supervision of the contract, not supervision of the people who are performing the work. This latter is the responsibility of contractors themselves and the distinction must be clearly understood by all who are involved.

Before plunging into a discussion of contract supervision, however, it might be useful to say a few words about the contractor's supervision of his or her own work-force.

9.2 THE CONTRACTOR

The contractor has agreed to carry out such works as are described in the Specification and in order to do this he or she will be expected to provide an adequate work-force. This work-force will include supervisory staff and management back-up, commensurate with the size of the contract.

If the contract is a small one, requiring only three or four operatives on site for most of the time, it is likely that one of them will be designated as leader of the team, answerable to the contractor or his manager. Such a person will be equivalent to the chargehand or working foreman as encountered in Local Government service.

Larger operations, involving two or more site gangs, may have a chargehand for each gang with a foreman having overall responsibility for the whole contract.

Whatever the size of the contract and irrespective of the number of persons on site, there should be one individual with overall responsibility for the contract works and this person should be identified at an early stage, possibly at the pre-contract meeting. He or she will be authorized to accept instructions, concerning the day-to-day running of the contract, from the Supervising Officer, and have the power to see that they are carried out by the work-force at their disposal. The extent of their authority will depend upon their position and status in the firm and is entirely a matter for the contractor to decide. At the very least they should be in a position to liaise with the Supervising Officer on matters concerning the daily work, to direct and supervise the work-force and generally to represent the contractor's interest with regard to practical matters on site.

9.3 THE SUPERVISING OFFICER

Turning now to the supervision of the contract from the point of view of the client or employer, the Supervising Officer is the most obvious person involved and it is he or she who will bear most of the responsibility for the operation of the contract. They should be named in the Specification and should make themselves known to the contractor's representative at an early stage.

The Supervising Officer's principal function is to represent the interests of the client and to ensure the smooth running of the contract from his or her point of view. Accordingly, the Supervising Officer should be fully experienced in the technical aspects of the contract and possess a good working knowledge of the contract site, including its previous maintenance history. He or she should fully understand their Authority's requirements with regard to the standard of work and have sufficient forcefulness of character to ensure that it is obtained. They will be fully conversant with the Specification and able to interpret its requirements in a sensible, fair and straightforward manner.

The Supervising Officer's administrative role will include the regular assessment of the progress of the contract and the authorization of Interim Payments, the keeping of such records as are required to service the contract and the maintenance of cost records. He or she will issue supplementary instructions to the contractor and initiate any Variation Orders which may be required.

He or she will almost certainly be involved in communication with the general public, dealing with residents' complaints and requests. This will, of course, be particularly relevant where the contract is concerned with the maintenance of housing-associated landscape. He or she may, occasionally, be required to attend residents' meetings and explain their Authority's policies with regard to matters of grounds maintenance.

The Supervising Officer will also have some input into the formulation of Specifications for new contracts, and his or her comments, based on practical experience of situations which may have arisen in the past, will provide a useful basis for any future modifications of the Specification.

In all but the smallest contracts, the Supervising Officer will be assisted in his or her daily supervision of the site work by some person or persons with delegated powers – the Supervising Officer's Representatives.

9.4   THE SUPERVISING OFFICER'S REPRESENTATIVE

The Supervising Officer's Representative may variously be termed a Contract Inspector, Clerk of Works, Supervising Foreman or some such similar title. For the sake of brevity, he or she will be referred to in these pages as 'the Inspector', although this is perhaps not the most apt designation, for as we will see, the duties cover a great deal more than this name might suggest.

The Inspector's responsibilities will be to liaise between the Supervising Officer and the contractor's on-site foreman, and by his daily presence on the contract site, to provide a direct front-line link between contractor and client. The Inspector will be authorized by the Supervising Officer to act on his or her behalf with regard to the day-to-day supervision of the contract and thus be able to relieve the Supervising Officer of a great deal of minor but nevertheless important detail.

The Inspector's duties will be many and varied. To carry them out effectively he or she will need to be aware of the contractor's working programme. He or she may well liaise with the contractor's foreman from time to time, in drawing up a programme of site work for the weeks ahead. At the very least, the Inspector needs to know when the contractor will be on site and the nature of the work he or she will be doing, in order to utilize his or her own time to maximum advantage. The Inspector will constantly check that the contractor is keeping up with the programme in so far as weather and site conditions allow. Some of the maintenance operations will require to be performed at particular times of the year, or at stated frequencies, and it is important that these times are adhered to. Occasionally circumstances may make it impossible to keep to the prescribed regime and the Inspector may then authorize suitable alternatives and guide the contractor in rearranging the programme of work accordingly.

The standard of work will be under continuous surveillance and must never be allowed to fall below that required by the Specification. The first few weeks of a new contract are vital in this respect, as it is then that the Inspector will establish the standards required and ensure that the contractor appreciates what is acceptable and what is not. If inferior work is allowed to be performed in the early stages, without demur on the part of the Inspector, it is very difficult to correct this at a later time. Any shortcomings in this respect should be brought to the attention of the contractor without delay.

The Inspector, with his or her superior knowledge of the contract area, should ensure that no part of the site is being overlooked. It sometimes happens that odd corners tend to get neglected, particularly if the contractor is unfamiliar with the contract area. The Inspector will be aware of the places where this is liable to happen and should ensure that such omissions are brought to the contractor's attention as soon as they are noted.

Another important aspect of the work is the maintenance of the safe working practices and compliance with the Health and Safety Regulations. The Specification will have something to say about this and the Inspector must ensure that the contractor is aware of its requirements and is complying with them. This is particularly important where machinery is involved or when pesticides are being used.

The Pesticide Regulations require that Certificates of Competence be held by persons using herbicides and other chemicals and an important part of the Inspector's job will be to check that certificate holders are present and in a position to supervise the operation of others in accordance with the requirements of the Regulations. The Inspector should also ensure that appropriate records are kept by the contractor, of all pesticide operations, and that copies are regularly transmitted to the Supervising Officer.

One of the few occasions when the Inspector is entitled to instruct members of the contractor's staff directly, is when they are seen to be doing something likely to be dangerous, either to themselves or to others. In such circumstances, if the contractor's foreman or person in charge is not present, it is the Inspector's duty to point out the danger and instruct the operatives to use safe working practices, or if this is not immediately possible or practicable, to order them to stop work immediately and report to their foreman. In this situation the Inspector should then seek out the contractor's foreman and inform him of the circumstances, at the earliest possible opportunity.

It may be that the Inspector is empowered to authorize additional works, of a minor nature, over and above the works required by the contract itself. In such cases, having identified the nature of the work required, he or she will initiate the raising of an order and instruct the contractor accordingly. When the additional work has been completed, the Inspector will certify the subsequent invoice before payment. Such items may take the form of replacement planting or minor landscape modifications or may simply be one of the normal maintenance operations repeated at a greater frequency than required by the contract terms.

If the contract is operated in such a way as to require the regular measurement of work it is the Inspector's responsibility to make such measurements as are required and to agree them with the contractor on site.

It may be necessary to issue materials to the contractor from time to time and the Inspector will normally be the person to authorize such issues. On the other hand, if the contractor is supplying the materials, the Inspector will check that they are of the right type and quality for the work in hand. This may entail sampling for subsequent analysis by the appropriate department.

Not all the Inspector's duties will involve direct dealings with the maintenance contractor. From time to time he or she will liaise with residents and members of the public in dealing with complaints or providing information. It is here that the Inspector's qualities of tact and diplomacy may be called upon as he or she will sometimes find themselves involved as an intermediary between the contractor and some third party.

To be completed and presented to the Manager by 21st of each month.

LMCS .... Name................. Contractor......................... Month ....

I am/am not* satisfied with the standard achieved   * (delete one or other).

Signed.................................... Name (BLOCK LETTERS)............................

Date........................

Item	Good	Poor	Comments
General appearance			
Performance: high maintenance areas			
Grass cutting/open space			
Grass cutting/obstacles			
Grass edging			
Shrubs/weed control			
Shrubs/pruning			
Sight lines/footpaths			
Climbers/weed control			
Climbers/supports/ties			
Hedges/weed control			
Hedge cutting			
Trees/stakes/ties/guys			
Trees/pruning (inc. adventitious growth)			
Trees basal herbicide			
Mature trees and hedges			
Hard surfaces			
Litter and rubbish			
Landscape depots internal			
Landscape depots external			

Other factors — including Health and Safety, professional/technical ability, time of operations.

Figure 9.1 Contract Inspector's check-list

The Inspector should be polite but not subservient, firm, but not arrogant, and should deal fairly with both sides when involved in any dispute involving a resident and the maintenance contractor. If the contractor is deemed to have been at fault the matter should be brought to his or her attention with a view to obtaining satisfactory recompense for the aggrieved person. At other times the Inspector will support the contractor when it is clear that he or she is not responsible for the problem and in this way will gain the contractor's respect as a fair-minded person.

In all of this, the Inspector must be careful not to usurp the authority of the Supervising Officer, who has the ultimate responsibility for supervision of the contract. The Inspector will be acting for the Supervising Officer and representing him or her in the matters of the day, but should be well aware of the extent and limits of the powers delegated to him or her by their superior officer.

The Inspector will no doubt be required to make regular reports to the Supervising Officer and certainly all disputes and differences of opinion should be reported without delay so that the Supervising Officer may be kept fully informed of the current situation.

With regard to the regular checking of the progress of the works, some form of simple check-list might be found useful. A typical example of such a list will be found in Figure 9.1. This form of regular progress report will serve as an early warning system for the Supervising Officer, enabling him or her to decide when their personal intervention is required, as well as providing a written record of the progress of the contract works.

It will be clear from the foregoing that the Contract Inspector will have much with which to occupy his or her time on site. Just how much work can he or she reasonably be expected to do? An Inspector's workload is difficult to establish and will vary according to a number of factors. Principal among these is the nature of the contract itself. Clearly, some maintenance contracts will be more demanding than others in this respect. As a rough guide, an Inspector may be expected to cover work up to an annual value of about £300 000 if the sites are compact and the work is of an intensive and demanding nature. The figure will vary, however, with the nature of the contract work and the amount of travelling involved between sites.

9.5 CONCLUSION

Contract supervision must be of a high standard if the contract is to succeed, and all involved in it must be carefully selected for their experience, their professionalism and the qualities which they can bring to bear. The cost of providing such supervision is a legitimate overhead and is likely to be recouped many times over in terms of a trouble-free and satisfactory performance.

CHAPTER 10

Schedules of Rates

10.1 THE NEED FOR A SCHEDULE

Most of the preceding pages of this book have been concerned
with the fixed-price term contract, whereby the contractor takes
total responsibility for all the work required within a prescribed
area for a fixed period of time, for an agreed lump-sum
payment. Not all the work of the Parks Department is capable
of being so neatly packaged, however.

From time to time, on the contract site, unexpected items of
work crop up which, because of their unplanned nature, have
not been included in the original contract. Such things as
vandalism, extreme weather conditions, natural wear and tear,
VIPs' visits and minor modifications to landscape layout in the
light of current conditions, can all result in additional unforeseen work.

In all but the most trivial cases, this work will not be absorbed
in the maintenance contract, as the contractor will not have
included for it in his or her tender. Consequently, it must be
regarded as a variation, and priced separately to the main
contract.

Similar situations can arise in areas which are not under
contract maintenance, and here the DLO will be expected to
deal with them. If this is not possible, or is inconvenient, some
other method must be found to perform the necessary work.

It is in circumstances such as these that the Schedule of Rates
will be found invaluable.

10.2 DESCRIPTION OF THE SCHEDULE

The Schedule of Rates is not a contract in itself, but may give
rise to many small contracts in the course of its operation.

Under this system a number of contractors are invited to submit their unit rates against a list of individual items of work. Such work may be required at any time, in any reasonable quantity and at any place, within the defining limits of the Specification. No guarantee is given that any work will be required but, if and when it is, a specific order will be raised and the contractual terms and conditions which accompany the Schedule will then apply.

The choice of contractor for a particular piece of work will be made on the basis of price and availability. It will not always be possible to utilize the lowest rate submitted, as that particular contractor may not be immediately available just at the time that he or she is required. If the work is urgent then it may be necessary to go to the next in order, even though it may mean paying slightly more, to get the work done.

It will be realized that no one contractor is likely to submit the lowest rates for all items on the Schedule. Consequently, different firms are likely to be selected for different types of work, according to the tenders submitted. This will result in a share-out of the available work, with a number of different firms being employed on different tasks, each probably of just a few hundred pounds in value on each occasion. Cumulatively, however, the value of the total work in any one year may amount to several thousand pounds.

The items to be listed on the Schedule may include all the many individual operations which are encountered in normal grounds maintenance, whether of a horticultural or arbori-cultural nature. Not all contractors will price everything; firms should be encouraged to submit rates only for those items that they are equipped to do. Day work rates may be included in order to cover any work that may not be individually priced.

Contractors who are involved in term contracts should be given the opportunity to price the Schedule of Rates and this can then be applied to variations on the contract. Term contractors should always be given the opportunity to carry out any additional work that may be required on their sites, provided that their rates are competitive and that their normal contract work is up to date.

The Schedule of Rates is a useful device for introducing new contractors, particularly the small local firms, to the harsh com-petitive world of contract grounds maintenance. Having carried out two or three small one-off jobs on a Schedule of Rates basis, experience is gained and confidence is built up, which might entitle the firm to be considered for inclusion on a tender list for a small term contract at a later date.

10.3   ANALYSIS OF THE SCHEDULE

The statistical analysis of the rates submitted under a Schedule presents some problems, due to the diverse nature of the items to be considered and the very large number of separate rates attached to each. If the Schedule contains fifty different items and returns are made by some forty contractors, both figures being not unreasonable, we can finish up with two thousand different items of data to be considered.

Unlike the fixed term contract, where we simply have to examine five figures and select the lowest, the Schedule of Rates involves a considerable amount of computational work if we are to interpret the Schedule in a way that is meaningful to those who use it. It should not be beyond the wit of some computer buff to devise a program to handle this and to produce the required final results, but failing this, recourse must be made to manual methods of analysis.

It is, of course, not practicable to place the tenderers in rank order, overall. The contractor who produces the lowest rates for grass-cutting items might prove to be expensive with shrub planting. The most competitive price for shrub planting might be submitted by the firm whose rates for hedge trimming are high, and so on. The permutations are endless.

The acceptable solution is to consider each of the separate items as an individual case and analyse the rates for that particular item before moving on to the next. This will enable average rates to be calculated for each item and contractors can then be listed as above or below the average in each case.

If this is done, it will generally be found that most, if not all, the tenderers will be below average on at least some items, notwithstanding that their rates for others may be high. On this basis, all contractors who have submitted their rates and have something to offer within the Schedule, should be accepted for possible use. Only those whose rates are above average on all items should be rejected, and these are likely to be few in number.

A recommended procedure for the manual processing of Schedule of Rates is as follows.

Item No.	Unit	Contractors					No. of rates
		A	B	C	D	E	
1	Hectare	35·00	13·00	19·50	25·00	12·00	5
2	Hectare	45·00	18·00	17·50	25·00		4
3	Hectare	45·00	20·00	20·00	25·00	18·00	5
4	100 m²	0·55	0·66	0·35	0·24	1·60	5
5	100 m²	1·90			1·20	0·85	3

(a)

Item No.	Unit	Contractors					No. of rates
		A	B	C	D	E	
1	Hectare	5	2	3	4	1	5
2	Hectare	4	2	1	3		4
3	Hectare	5	2	2	4	1	5
4	100 m²	3	4	2	1	5	5
5	100 m²	3			2	1	3

(b)

Figure 10.1 Analysis of Schedule: (a) Chart A: tendered rates; (b) Chart B: ordered tenders

10.3.1 Step 1

Allocate a code letter to each contractor – A, B, C etc. Thereafter all the tenderers are referred to by their code letter. This simplifies the column headings on the charts and forms used in the analysis of the data and also helps to reduce the possibility of bias towards any one contractor unconsciously creeping in, as the person who is analysing the rates will not know to whom they belong until after the analysis has been completed.

10.3.2 Step 2

Prepare a chart as in Figure 10.1(a)(Chart A) with the contractors across the top and the Schedule items down the side. Commencing with contractor A, insert all his or her proffered rates against the appropriate item numbers in the first column of the chart.

In the example given, the contractor has tendered £35.00 per hectare for item 1, £45.00 for items 2 and 3, 55p per 100 m^2 for item 4 and £1.40 for item 5.

Repeat for contractor B. This contractor has not submitted a rate for item 5 so the appropriate box on the chart is left blank.

Continue with each contractor in turn until all have been recorded. Count the number of rates received for each item and insert the totals in the right-hand column. In the example, five rates have been received for item 1, four for item 2, five each for items 3 and 4 and only three for item 5.

The example in Figure 10.1 covers the rates submitted by only five contractors on a Schedule containing just five items. In practice, of course, there would be considerably more items on the Schedule and a much larger number of tenderers. It will be found convenient to prepare the chart on a large sheet of graph paper (A1 size) extended, if necessary, by taping additional pieces on, using scotch tape.

10.3.3 Step 3

Prepare a second chart (Chart B, Figure 10.1(b)) similar to the first list, this time inserting the ordinal numbers of the rates instead of the rates themselves. These can be found by inspection of Chart A. The lowest rate for any item will have rank 1, the second lowest will be 2 and so on. Thus, for item 1 in the example, the lowest rate is £12.00 offered by contractor E, so the number 1 goes in the box under E. Next comes a rate of £13.00 submitted by contractor B so number 2 is inserted in column B. Contractor C is third with £14.50, fourth is D with £25.00 and the highest, fifth, is that of contractor A with £35.00, so 5 is inserted in the A column.

Insert the total number of rates in the right-hand column, in this case: 5 and check that this agrees with the corresponding figure in Chart A. Continue in this way with each horizontal line in turn until the chart is complete.

Item No.	Lowest rates		Highest rates		No. of Rates Rec'd	Average (median) rates	Tenderers (in rank order)
a	b		c		d	e	f
1	E	12·00	A	35·00	5	14·50	E B C | D A
2	C	17·50	A	45·00	4	21·50	C B | D A
3	E	18·00	A	45·00	5	20·00	E B/C | D A
4	D	0·24	E	1·60	5	0·55	D C A | B E
5	E	0·85	A	1·40	3	1·20	E D | A

Figure 10.2 Analysis of Schedule: Chart C: statistical analysis

Note that, for item 3, we have two similar rates vying for second place, so there is no number 3 in this case.

10.3.4 Step 4

The final stage of the analysis is illustrated in Figure 10.2.

Prepare Chart C with column headings as shown and list the item numbers in the left-hand column.

Columns b, c and d require little explanation, the data being obtained by inspection from Charts A and B. For each item, identify the contractor with the lowest and highest rates and insert the code letter on the left and the relevant rate on the right in each of columns b and c. Column c contains the average of the rates received for each item. The median is the most appropriate type of average to use as the lowest and/or highest rates are often extreme compared with the others. In the case of item 1, where we have five rates all different, this will be the third rate, which is £14.50.

Item 2 presents an even number of rates, so the median is found by taking the mean of the two middle values, i.e.

$$\frac{18.00 + 25.00}{2} = 21.50$$

In item 3, the middle rate is the third, which is represented by either B or C as these are equal. Items 4 and 5 are straight-forward, being the third and second rates, respectively.

Finally, in column f, the contractors are listed in rank order against each item. Note that, against item 3, B/C indicates that these two contractors have submitted the same rate and are thus of equal rank. It could equally have been written as C/B.

The vertical line separates those rates which are below or equal to the average, from those which are above it. Thus, in item 1, we have three contractors whose rates could be recommended as below the average rate for that particular job, and two who would not normally be used, as their rates are above the average. A useful device is to enter the below-average contractors in green and the above-average ones in red. This gives an immediate indication of preferred tenders and renders the use of the vertical line unnecessary.

Chart C may then be used as the basis on which to prepare the tender report, using whatever information is required for this purpose.

Although intended principally as a method of facilitating the choice of contractor, based on price, for any particular kind of work, the results of this analysis will be found useful for other purposes. These include the preparation of estimates and the study of market trends, to name but two.

CHAPTER 11

Contract documentation

Contract administration inevitably generates a considerable amount of paperwork. Much of this takes the form of standard documentation of a repetitive nature, whether concerned with the origination of the contracts or their subsequent management. The most important of these, the contract specification, has already been discussed and this chapter looks at some of the other forms and documents that are required.

11.1 THE CONTRACT FILE

Although not strictly a 'document' in its own right, the contract file is a useful device, which precedes all other forms of documentation.

At the start of the contract season, the contracts to be arranged will be identified and each will be given a name and a contract number. A file should then be opened for each one and eventually this will contain everything relating to that particular contract from its inception, right throughout its life, to the end of the contract period. In this way a complete history of each contract will be available in a single folder and this will greatly facilitate the administration of the contract from start to finish.

For this purpose, a wallet file, of foolscap size, with clip for securing papers, will be found suitable. A further refinement is to use different coloured files for different types of contract or for different contract years.

Initially, the file will contain check-lists and information concerning the preparation of the contract, including copies of all information sent out to tenderers. It will include a copy of the Specification, any plans or drawings and copies of all other relevant information. The progress of the tendering will be recorded and copies of all letters and documents included.

Once the contract has been let, all relevant material concerning its progress will go into the file. This will include copies of all correspondence, reports and instructions, variation orders, payment certificates and other appropriate information, thus providing a complete record of the contract throughout its life.

11.2 THE CONTRACT CHECK-LIST

The procedure which culminates in the letting of a contract involves many separate operations and can extend over a period of several months. When, as is often the case, a number of contracts are being prepared concurrently it is easy to lose track of what stage each one has reached. This can result in confusion, with time wasted in back-tracking to determine what should be done next with each one. Even worse, there is the danger of omitting some vital stage, or failing to meet a deadline, which can throw the whole programme out of sequence.

It is essential to plan ahead and programme the whole operation, allocating dates for completion of the various stages, and to ensure that the programme is rigidly adhered to, in order that nothing should be overlooked and all the preliminary work is finalized well in advance of the contract start dates. A useful aid for this is the contract check-list.

The contract check-list is a list of all the separate operations required, arranged in the order in which they should be carried out. The list may be as simple or as detailed as required, but it is important that no vital stage be omitted. Each item may be marked off as it is completed, thus ensuring an up-to-date record, at all times, of the stage that the contract has reached.

The list might take the form of a line-by-line description of the individual processes with a column for marking off the completed stages, or a flow chart might be used similar to that illustrated in Figure 11.1. The check-list will normally be the first document to go into the contract file and will be used throughout the preparation of the contract to record its progress.

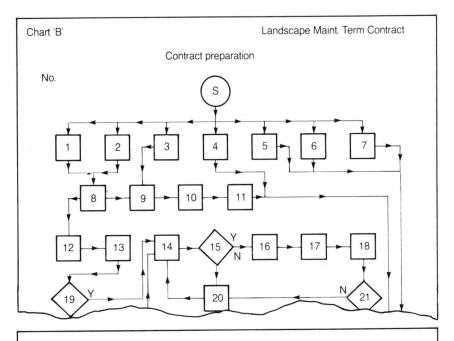

Chart 'B'   Landscape Maint. Term Contract

Contract preparation

No.

Chart 'B'	Key to operations
1	Obtain Landscape Summaries
2	Copy master Specification
3	Identify drawing numbers
4	Obtain contract drawings
5	Prepare Forms of Tender
6	Prepare specimen Depot Agreements
7	Prepare Supplementary Schedules (if required)
8	Prepare Landscape Schedules
9	Prepare Contract Specifications
10	Send Specifications for printing
11	Obtain printed Specifications
12	Calculate Provisional Estimate
13	Compile provisional tender list
14	

Figure 11.1 Contract progress check-list

11.3 INTENTION TO TENDER

The Intention to Tender Form (ITT), referred to briefly in Chapter 8, is used before sending out the Tender Packages. Its use can save the embarrassment of receiving an insufficient number of tenders which may result in the abandonment of the contract with the consequent need to re-tender.

The ITT may consist of a simple returnable form with accompanying explanatory letter (see Figure 11.2). On the form contractors will be required to confirm their intention to submit a valid tender, or alternatively, to state the reason for declining, if such be their decision. The form should be accompanied by some rough indication of the type of contract and its size in order to assist the contractor in making his or her decisions. This may be done in a number of ways, e.g:

1. By giving an indication of the probable value of the contract:
   'Tenders will be expected within the range of £30 000 to £35 000'
2. By stating the approximate area:
   'An area of parkland consisting of some 25 ha.'
3. By attaching a Bill of Quantities.
4. By giving some other indication of size:
   'An area of housing associated landscape on adjoining estates, comprising approximately 1500 dwellings.'

A date should be given by which the ITT should be returned. Two full weeks should be adequate for this. The ITT's should be sent out to all contractors on the Tender List. If all are returned with an affirmative answer the Tender Packages may be sent out with confidence. If a contractor states that he or she does not wish to tender on this occasion, however, then a substitute can be selected to take their place.

There are a number of valid reasons why a contractor might not wish to tender for a particular contract, the most usual one being that his or her resources have already been allocated to other contracts.

11.4 INSTRUCTIONS FOR TENDERING

The Instructions for Tendering should be clearly set out on a

To: The Landscape Maintenance Contract Programmer
        Milton Keynes Development Corporation
        7 North Tenth Street
        Central Milton Keynes MK9 3DU

Notice of Intention to Tender

* I wish to be given the opportunity to tender for Landscape/Forestry
  Maintenance Contracts and/or Schedule of Rates as follows:

* I do not wish to tender on this occasion for the following reasons:

* Please cross out whichever does NOT apply.

Signed .... Date ....

Company ....

To be received at the above address not later than:

Figure 11.2 Intention to tender

Instructions for Tendering

LMCS/467

1. Inspection of contract site
It is a condition of Tendering that the Tenderer shall visit the Contract Site prior to submitting his Tender in the company of the SO or his representative in order to satisfy himself of the site conditions prevailing and to ascertain the full requirements of the Contract. (See Clause 5 of Bill No. 1 — Preliminary Investigation.) The Employer reserves the right to refuse to accept any Tender where such a visit has not taken place.

2. Provision of documents
Tenderers will be supplied with TWO blank copies of the Form of Tender; one is to be submitted to the Milton Keynes Development Corporation, and the other copy to be retained by the Tenderer.

3. Acceptance of tender
The Tender should be made on the Form of Tender provided with/in the Contract Documents which should be submitted fully priced and totalled in BLACK INK. Unit rates and prices must be quoted in pounds and decimal fractions of a pound. Such fractions need not be restricted to any specific number of decimal places.

The Tender is to cover the whole of the Contract works as stated in the documentation provided.

No UNAUTHORIZED alterations or additions should be made to the Form of Tender or to any other of the Contract Documents; IF ANY SUCH ALTERATION IS MADE OR IF THESE INSTRUCTIONS ARE NOT FULLY COMPLIED WITH, THE TENDER MAY BE REJECTED.

4. Date for return
No Tender will be accepted unless it is received in the enclosed envelope, addressed to the Milton Keynes Development Corporation, at the address shown on the label.

The envelope shall not bear any name or mark indicating the sender and shall be received in the Development Corporation Offices not later than 12.00 pm on Monday 5 December 1988.

5. Tenderer's expenses
The Employer does not bind himself to accept the lowest or any Tender nor will be held responsible for, or pay for, expenses or losses which may be incurred by the Tenderer in the preparation of his Tender.

6. Additions to the tender
Should any additions, amendments or alterations to the Contract Documents as issued to Tenderers be deemed to be necessary prior to the date for submission of Tender, these will be issued to the Tenderers in the form of a Supplementary Schedule and form part of the Contract Document.

Figure 11.3 Instructions for tendering

separate document which forms part of the Tender Package. They should not be written into the Specifications; this being the Contract Document, it only comes into force when the contract is let, by which time it is too late to worry about tendering procedures.

Figure 11.3 indicates a suitable form of wording which may be modified to suit local requirements. As with other similar documents, the Instructions for Tendering may be prepared as a 'master' with blank spaces for names and dates etc. This can then be photocopied and the relevant details completed for each particular contract as required.

11.5 FORM OF TENDER

The Tender Form may also be produced as a standard 'master'. Figure 11.4 shows such a form after customizing by completion of the blanks for a specific contract.

The breakdown of the total tender sum is optional and may include whatever subdivisions are required. Instead of using geographical areas it might be appropriate to split according to the operations required, e.g:

> Grass maintenance ....
> Tree maintenance ....
> Shrub maintenance ....
> etc.

11.6 NON-TENDER FORM

The purpose and use of the Non-tender Form has been described in Chapter 8. Figure 11.5 provides a suitable form of wording for this document.

11.7 SUPPLEMENTARY SCHEDULES

It sometimes happens that amendments to a contract become necessary after the Specification has been printed. This may be due to unforeseen changes on the contract area, new legislation or simply the correction of errors in the documentation. If it is

FORM OF TENDER

Tender for: Landscape Maintenance Work at: FISHERMEAD,
OLDBROOK
AND SPRINGFIELD

Contract No: LMCS/467

To: Milton Keynes Development Corporation
Saxon Court, 502 Avebury Boulevard,
Central Milton Keynes MK9 3HS

Sirs

I/We having read the Conditions of Contract and Bill of Quantities delivered to
me/us and having examined the drawings referred to therein do hereby offer to
execute and complete in accordance with the Conditions of Contract the whole of
the works described during the whole of the TWO year Contract Period from 1 April
1989 to 31 March 1991 for the sum of

....

(£   ) The above mentioned tender price is made up as follows:

Two-Year Prices

Fishermead ....
Oldbrook Housing ....
Oldbrook Sheltered Housing ....
Springfield Housing ....
Springfield Sheltered Housing ....

Materials ....

Two-Year total (to agree with tender sum above)   _____

£ _____

We hereby declare that I/We have not communicated the amount of any proposed
tender for these works to any person other then the person calling for this tender
and have not adjusted the amount of this tender in accordance with any agreement
or arrangement with any person other than the person calling for this tender.

SEE OVER . . . .

Figure 11.4 Form of tender: (a) front; (b) reverse

I/we agree that when called upon to do so we will execute a formal Agreement embodying the terms of our above offer and that until such Agreement is prepared and executed this offer and your unconditional written acceptance of it will constitute a binding contract between us as to the rate, prices and other terms and conditions upon and subject to which we will during the period aforesaid provide and carry out the said landscaping maintenance.

Dated this .... Day of ....

Company Name ....

Address ....

....

....

....

Signature ....

Position in Firm ....

Witness ....

Witness ....

NON-TENDER FORM
LMCS/467

FISHERMEAD, OLDBROOK, SPRINGFIELD

If for any reason, you do NOT wish to tender for the above, please complete this form and return to:

R. M. Chadwick
Programmer: Landscape Contract Maintenance
MKDC
7 North Tenth Street
Central Milton Keynes
MK9 3DU

TO BE RETURNED BEFORE THE CLOSING DATE AS STATED:

12.00 pm on MONDAY 5 DECEMBER 1988

I do NOT wish to tender for the above contract for the following reason(s):

Signed ....

Name of Company ....

....

NB: Failure to return this form (in the event of NON-Tendering) could result in your name being removed from our tender list.

Figure 11.5 Non-tender form

too late to alter the Specification this sort of information is best sent out as a 'Supplementary Schedule'. This will be included in the tender package if possible and will form part of the contract documentation.

If it becomes necessary to issue a Supplementary Schedule after the Tender Package has been despatched then a judgement must be taken, having regard to the remaining time left for tendering, as to whether this procedure may be used.

11.8 TENDER REPORTS

Once the tenders for a contract have been received, they should be carefully validated and the successful tenderer identified, as described in Chapter 8. A report should then be drawn up for submission to the Officer, or committee, having the authority to approve the letting of the contract.

The exact form which the Tender Report will take will be determined by custom and practice of the Authority concerned. In all cases, however, and irrespective of its length and layout, the report should include all the relevant information necessary to enable a competent decision to be made concerning the future of the contract. This will include:

1. The contract name and number
2. Length of the contract
3. Type of contract, e.g. Verge Maintenance, Sportsground Maintenance etc
4. The estimate value
5. Names of the companies invited to tender
6. List of tenders received, in size order, with names of companies submitting them
7. Reason for any non-tenders, if known
8. A statement concerning the validity, and absence of qualifications, of the tenders
9. The recommended tender
10. If any but the lowest tender is recommended then a full explanation should be given
11. Any other relevant information

Milton Keynes Development Corporation

Landscape Maintenance Contract Section

VARIATION ORDER

CONTRACT:

CONTRACTOR:

The following variation will apply to the above mentioned
Contract with effect from the below date.

VARIATION:

FINANCIAL IMPLICATION

The financial implication of this order will be to increase/decrease the Annual
Contract Price by £ ....

Current ACP : £ ....   Amended ACP : £ ....

Signed: ....
(Supervising Officer)

Date: ....

Figure 11.6 Variation order

11.9 VARIATION ORDERS

If the contract allows for variations then it will be found useful to prepare a standard form for use on appropriate occasions.

Variation Orders are issued by the SO and should always be in writing, signed and dated. Figure 11.6 indicates the typical layout of such a document. It will be seen that it includes a description of the variation, with reference to the appropriate drawings if necessary, together with the financial implications.

The Variation Order has the effect of increasing or decreasing the amount of work required by the contract and usually results in an adjustment of the Contract Price. For this reason, copies should go to the Finance Department as well as to the contractor concerned.

11.10 PAYMENT CERTIFICATES

Payment to the contractor may be made in two ways. If the contract is based on a Schedule of Rates, the employer will raise orders for specific parcels of work from time to time. When the contractor has completed the work on an order, he or she will submit an invoice for payment.

Alternatively, the works may be carried out according to a previously agreed programme and interim payments will be made. This implies the issue of Interim Certificates and ultimately a Final Certificate when the contract is completed.

The frequency and amount of interim payments will be stated in the Specification. It is common to make twelve such payments, at monthly intervals during the contract year, although fewer payments at longer intervals may be specified if desired. The simplest method is to make all the payments of equal value, i.e. annual contract sum is divided by the number of payments to be made and the resultant figure becomes the amount to be certified on each occasion. This greatly simplifies the administrative work required in preparing the certificates and usually works to the client's advantage in as much as the contract is forward loaded, due to the bulk of the work being performed during the first few months of the contract year.

The Interim Certificate should state the total amount due to date, the amount previously certified and the balance due. If

Interim Certificate

I certify that under the Terms of Contract for the works known as

Contract No.
Contract Sum £
Instalment No.
Date of valuation
Date of Issue

an Interim Payment as detailed below is due

from the Employer
of

Milton Keynes Development Corporation
Wavendon Tower, Wavendon
Milton Keynes MK17 8LX

to the Contractor
of

Gross amount £
Retention £

Net amount £
Previously certified £

BALANCE £

Amount due
for payment

£

Statement of Supervising Officer:

I have inspected the works and am satisfied that the Contractor has fulfilled his obligations under the terms of the Contract, up to the date of valuation.

Signed:

Supervising Officer

STATEMENT OF RETENTION

Total monies retained on this contract to date

£

DISTRIBUTION ☐ Employer ☐ LMCM
Supervising Officer ☐ Contractor

Figure 11.7 Payment certificate

any money is to be retained this will also be noted and VAT if appropriate will be added to the final amount due. See Figure 11.7.

The certificate will be signed by the Supervising Officer (SO), who before doing so, will have satisfied himself or herself that all work under the contract has been completed to date and is of the required standard. If such is not the case, the SO may delay the issue of the certificate until such time as the works have been brought up to date, but this sanction must be used with care and only as a last resort in the case of nonperformance or unsatisfactory performance.

The Final Certificate, as its name suggests, authorizes the final payment under the contract. As such it is issued at the end of the contract period or at the end of the retention period if applicable.

Before issuing the Final Certificate, a careful check should be made that all is in order and that the final figures balance correctly. The amount due will take into account retention money (if any), the value of any Variation Orders that may have been issued and any authorized stoppages that may have been agreed. If payment is due for any materials supplied by the contractor this will no doubt be separately invoiced but, if not, then the amounts outstanding may be included in the final sum.

11.11 OTHER CONTRACT DOCUMENTATION

In the preceding pages we have discussed some of the more important documents which are likely to be required within the framework of the Grounds Maintenance Contract Section. There are, of course, many other items which will be required for general administrative purposes in connection with the normal running of the busy Contract Section.

For example, no mention has been made of the series of records used to record the details of the contractors themselves. Files may be kept for individual contractors which will contain applications for inclusion on the approved list, inventories of plant and machinery, references, financial information, copies of insurance documents and Tax Exemption Certificates, records of contracts offered and tender results and other relevant matters. Standard forms and letters may be designed for many of these purposes.

All of these, and other matters of a more general administrative nature, can be safely left to the individual officer, to develop as occasion demands. The requirements, as always, will vary from one Authority to another and it would be profitless, if not presumptuous, for any one person to dictate how these matters should be arranged. Suffice it to say that records should be kept of all matters that are likely to be of use or importance at some later stage and these will embrace financial and costing, technical, administrative, trade information, statistical and other subjects.

The Contract Section thrives on information and it is surprising how much useful information can be gathered in only two or three years of operation. If properly filed so as to be readily accessible at all times, much of it may be fed back into the system and by this means, improve the efficiency and enable improvements as a result of experience to be incorporated.

Discrimination should be used when deciding what should be retained and for how long. We should beware of keeping records for records' sake. If it has not been necessary to consult a file within, say, the last five years, then throw it away or archive it. After all, we are in the business of maintaining grounds and – filing cabinets do not cut grass!

CHAPTER 12

The DLO as tenderer

Throughout the major part of this book the principal object has been to described how the Local Authority can arrange its contracts and manage its contractors. There are many who would say, however: 'That is not the main problem. Tell us how we can manage without private contractors. Tell us how we can win all the work for ourselves in order to preserve our Direct Labour Organizations at full strength and so continue to maintain our grounds in the way that we always have done.' It is time now to deal with this problem and to see if there is any way that such ends can be assured.

12.1 THE COMPETITIVE DLO

Competition is here to stay, the Local Government Act has ensured that. There is no legal way that an Authority can opt out of the Act's requirements and the only way that a DLO may continue to function is by proving its competitiveness in a competitive situation. There are several ways in which this might be done, but the particular way that the Act requires is by winning tenders. The question posed above therefore resolves itself into: 'How can we, acting to all intents and purposes as a contractor, in competition with other contractors, ensure that we will win all our contracts?'

This is the question that every contractor has been asking from time immemorial and no-one has yet come up with a satisfactory answer. The truth is, of course, that in a competitive situation there can be no guarantees. The contractor does not exist who has never lost a tender. There is no way, in fair competition, that any contractor will always win everything that he or she goes for. If this were not so, there would be one very rich contractor and all the others would be out of business.

Having said this, it is certainly true that some are more successful than others and this is a reflection of their management and business skills as well as of their technical ability.

If the DLO is to function as a contractor they must recognize at the outset that they are not going to win all their bids. There is no reason why they should not be at least as successful as the average contractor, however, and in many cases will be able to score a greater number of hits than most. The DLO has a number of advantages which, if used aright, will enable them to succeed against what might appear to be superior odds. Before looking at these, however, let us consider some of the more obvious problems, as these need to be recognized and counter measures devised, at an early stage.

12.2   PROBLEMS TO BE OVERCOME

The fact that there are problems and difficulties facing any Authority which wishes to keep its grounds maintenance in-house should not surprise us, nor need it cause undue concern. As we shall see, there are ways of dealing with them and, indeed, most Local Authorities are in a much stronger position to deal with them than are many of their competitors. It should be realized that every private contractor has his or her problems, albeit of a different nature, and in most cases they cannot bring to bear on them the sort of resources that are generally available within the organization of the average Local Authority.

Most of the problems facing the DLO in its efforts to prove its competitiveness can be classified as financial, ethical or practical in nature.

12.2.1   The financial problems

The question of oncost, or overhead rate, has already been touched on (Chapter 1) and this difficult problem must be resolved before any comparisons may be made with private sector costs.

In its simplest form the DLO hourly rate will be based on:

1. Wages and salaries
2. Materials and fuel

3. Departmental oncost
4. General overhead

The first and most difficult step is to remove the general overhead from the equation completely, after which the Departmental oncost will need to be pruned down to the absolute minimum, if financial parity is to be achieved with the private sector.

This first problem implies a different form of accounting and as such, requires the co-operation of the Finance Department. The basis for such a system will be to examine each item in turn and ask the question: 'If the DLO did not exist, would this cost still be recoverable?' If the answer is 'Yes', then it should not be included in the DLO hourly rate. If the answer is 'No', then that particular item, or at least the DLO's fair share of it, should be retained in the Department's overheads.

Next, it is necessary to examine the Departmental oncost and look for ways of reducing this to the minimum consistent with the need to maintain an efficient and well-run Department with conditions and facilities no less favourable than hitherto.

When this has been done, the resultant figure should be added to the cost of wages and salaries to give a total sum which can then be divided by the number of personnel to produce an hourly operating cost.

At this stage it would be wise to consider the question of residual costs. These are the costs which, while not generated directly by the DLO, are nevertheless considered to be a rightful charge against that Department.

If we imagine a situation where the DLO had been completely closed down, we might not expect any further operating costs to be charged to it. However, we would still receive complaints and queries from residents, OAPs would doubtless need help with their gardens, planning permissions might have landscape implications and school nature projects and visits from outside organizations would doubtless require some sort of input. All these and similar matters, which would normally be dealt with by the DLO, will require attention from somebody and thus will generate costs. In some cases the work could be handled by other Departments and some of it, no doubt, could be included in the maintenance contracts. There will always be a certain amount of this work, however, that can, logically, only be handled by the DLO and these items make up our 'residual costs'.

Due allowance must be made for these residuals as they will undoubtedly occur in one form or another and thus should be included in the Departmental oncost.

By the time that these words are being read, many Authorities will have completed the process of rationalizing their costs and will have arrived at a much more realistic hourly rate. This is still likely to be higher than the average contractor's rate, but fortunately there is a potential for further cost savings (enumerated below) which will go much of the way towards offsetting this.

Once the true cost of running the DLO has been established, consideration can then be given to the moral issues involved in tendering.

12.2.2   The ethical problems

If the DLO is to tender for contracts in competition with the private sector, then it follows that such tendering should not only be fair, but be seen to be fair by all concerned.

Consider first, the Contract Specification. It is possible to write a Specification in such a way as to make tendering by most private contractors extremely unattractive and impossibly expensive, while allowing the DLO to compete on favoured terms. Conversely, it could be written in such terms as to disbar the DLO from competing.

The first option, if consciously undertaken, is immoral and unproductive. Since there is no real competition, the result is a foregone conclusion and cannot truly be considered as a competitive tender situation. The second course is completely suicidal if it is intended that the DLO should have an opportunity to win contracts.

The only fair method of competitive tendering is to offer a contract on terms that are reasonable and likely to be acceptable to all the parties who are eligible to tender for it. If this is to include the DLO as well as private contractors, then this must be borne in mind when the Specification is drafted.

The next question to be considered is that of privileged information. All the tenderers should be given identical information concerning the contract in order that the tenders are comparable, thus enabling a decision to be made based on price alone. No tenderers should be in possession of information which is not available to their competitors and which would give them an unfair advantage in arranging their price.

It must be said that the Local Authority, and to a large extent the DLO itself, will be privy to a considerable amount of information that is unlikely to be available to the other tenderers, e.g.

(a)   The previous DLO cost of the work

Tenderers knowing the DLO cost of the contract work in a previous year would have an advantage, inasmuch as they would know what they had to beat. The successful tender might be expected to be marginally below the DLO cost in these circumstances.

(b)   The estimate

The contract estimate represents a figure perhaps 5–10% higher than the value of the successful tender.

(c)   The tender list

If tenderers know who their competitors are, they may well be able to form some idea of the magnitude of the tenders likely to be submitted by them. In any competition it helps to know the opposition.

(d)   Information about contractors

Over a period of time, the client gathers a considerable amount of trade information, including financial information, concerning the contractors, some of which is of a confidential nature. Coupled with (c) above, this can be of value in assessing the nature of the opposition.

It will be realized from the above that the DLO is likely to be in a more favourable position than its competitors on account of superior knowledge, not shared by the other tenderers. It is not suggested that the DLO would win on every occasion as a result of this, although they would certainly have a much better chance than the others. What is certain, however, is that the situation could not be regarded as one of true and fair competition, thus defeating the whole object of competitive tendering. Furthermore, it would only be a short time before the other tenderers realized their disadvantaged position and we would be likely to find more and more firms declining to tender in these circumstances.

One solution might be to offer the information held by the DLO to all the other tenderers, thus equalizing the position and thereby restoring the principle of fair competitive tendering. While this might be done with regard to items (a), (b) and (c); item (d) could not be made public as it includes confidential information concerning individual contractors.

The way that most Authorities have solved the problem of privileged information is to establish a separate 'Client Section', completely divorced from the DLO, to arrange and manage its contract work.

The Client Section will act for the Authority in all matters concerning contract grounds maintenance. They will arrange the contracts, prepare documentation, interview contractors, invite tenders and in due course make their recommendation for the letting of contracts. The Supervising Officer will be a member of the Client Section, as will be his or her inspecting officers, responsible for the supervision of the contracts. In all this, the DLO will be regarded as a potential contractor and will receive exactly the same treatment as any other contractor – no more and no less. The Client Section should operate under a code of conduct which should be publicized for all to see.

The DLO, for their part, will need to re-think their entire operation and if they are to regard themselves as a 'contractor section' will require to adjust their methods of working in order to comply with the constraints of contractual work. A change of attitudes at all levels will be called for and staff will need to be impressed with the need to operate in conformity with the contract specification and its requirements.

Potential work must be sought out, with neighbouring Authorities as well as their own, and decisions made as to which works they should tender. Tenders will then need to be compiled, taking into account not only the nature and amount of work required, but the terms and conditions under which they must work.

When the contract has been secured they will be required to carry out the works in a manner acceptable to the Supervising Officer concerned and to do so in accordance with the financial limits of the tender submitted. This will entail constant surveillance of all expenditure on the contract and the operation of a tight system of financial control throughout the whole operation.

Table 12.1 Responsibilities of Client and Contract Sections

Client Section	Contract Section (DLO)
Survey maintenance sites and prepare landscape summaries and drawings	Streamline organization and carry out any retraining considered necessary
Arrange contracts and prepare Bills of Quantities and contract drawings	Seek out potential work from own and neighbouring Authorities
Prepare specifications and all other contract documentation	Respond to advertisements and invitations
Prepare contract estimates	Inspect documentation of potential contract work
Publish necessary notices and advertisements as required by the Act	Decide whether or not to tender in specific cases
Compile select list of contractors and carry out all necessary screening	Prepare and submit tenders
Arrange for contract documentation to be made available for inspection by interested parties	Perform maintenance work on contracts awarded
Despatch tender documents to selected contractors	Prepare and submit cost statements and reports as required
Evaluate tenders and make recommendations	Review cost statements at regular intervals to ensure working to budget
Supervise contracts awarded and provide all necessary 'back-up'	
Authorize payments to contractors	

The various responsibilities of the Client and Contract Sections are summarized briefly in Table 12.1.

This method of working will go a long way towards satisfying the ethical objections to allowing the DLO to tender in competition with outside contractors and to ensure that no favouritism or bias is allowed to enter into the letting of the contracts.

12.2.3   Practical difficulties

At first sight there would appear to be a major problem which would arise as soon as the successful DLO wins its first contract. With whom is the contract to be made? A grounds maintenance contract requires two parties – a client Authority who sets it up and pays for it and the contractor who carries out the works. Since the DLO is part of the Authority and its staff are all directly employed by it, the client would appear to be making a contract with itself. It is difficult to imagine how such a unilateral contract could be operated.

The normal two-party Specification could not apply in these circumstances, as the Authority would be required to pay itself, supervise itself and maybe impose sanctions and penalties on itself if things went wrong. In the ultimate, it might even have to determine the contract and throw itself out if serious breach occurred. This is obviously ridiculous and a special Specification would have to be written in order to obviate these anomalies. This would not be the Specification against which the other tenderers had tendered, however, so technically, it would be a different contract. Fortunately, however, this problem is more imaginary than real.

In the event that a DLO is awarded a 'contract' as a result of a competitive tendering situation, they will operate under a works contract as defined by the Local Government Act. This is not the same as the contract that would be made by acceptance of a private contractor's tender. This latter is a normal bipartite contract in the legally accepted sense of the term and as such is governed by contract law. In this, one party (the Contractor) undertakes to perform certain work and/or supply certain services in return for a consideration provided by the other party (the Employer).

The works contract is not a contract in this sense. It cannot be, as the contractor and the employer are the same Authority; furthermore, as there is no consideration, no contract can be said to exist.

The position is that the DLO, by proving its competitiveness in competition, has won the right to carry out the works described in the contract documentation and may then do so according to the requirements of the Act. These requirements include that the DLO must operate throughout in accordance with the Specification and the conditions of contract, so far as they can be applied. It is also required that the works shall be performed within the tendered amount submitted by the DLO.

Thus, in performing a works contract, the DLO is bound by the requirements of the Act, not just by the conditions of contract. A consequence of this is that any failure by the DLO to honour its obligations, exposes the Authority to the likelihood of sanctions, as described in the Local Government Act.

12.3   THE DLO's ADVANTAGEOUS POSITION

As suggested above, the DLO has a number of advantages over the private contractor with regard to the preparation of the tender and the performance of the contract itself. Most of these are of a cost-saving nature and this will improve the DLO's chances of success in the competitive situation. These advantages may be considered under three headings, as follows.

12.3.1   Experience

Because of its previous experience, the DLO will have an intimate knowledge of the contract area. Not only will they be familiar with the geography of the site, but they will be aware of any problem areas and will know exactly what has to be done on any part of the site. This means that their assessment of the work is likely to be more accurate than others and the cost of preparing it will be reduced by omitting the need for site visits to assess the nature of the work required and the resources needed to carry it out.

12.3.2   Resources

The DLO will already have the staff, the machinery and equipment close at hand, ready to do the work. There will be no need to recruit and train new staff, or to purchase new plant and machinery and this will result in considerable cost savings which will be reflected in the tender.

A contractor would need to transfer key staff, recruit locally or appoint sub-contractors. It is also likely that he or she would purchase new mowing equipment and other plant for the contract and the cost of all these items would be included in their tender.

The DLO will already have appropriate depot and storage facilities on or near the contract site. A contractor would need to bring in, or hire, such facilities at a cost which again, would be included in his or her tender price.

12.3.3   Other advantages

The contractor would need to discover the standard of work acceptable to the Authority under the contract and this is usually a matter of trial and error over the first few weeks of the contract period.

The DLO, on the other hand, would be aware of what is acceptable from the start and this learning period would not be required. This would result in a better and more efficient performance of the contract from day one.

Finally, there is the question of profit. The DLO should add a minimum 5% to its tender to cover the profit element. Contractors, in most cases, will be operating to a considerably higher profit margin, as this is the principal reason for their being there. They may have shareholders to pay and will be expected to return an adequate margin to cover reinvestment and expansion in addition to other considerations.

There may be occasions when a low profit margin is acceptable to a contractor, but these are likely to apply mainly in the case of small local firms working on the basis of a Schedule of Rates. In most cases, the DLO will have a considerable advantage over the private contractor in that they will generally be operating at a much lower profit level and this will be favourably reflected in their tender price.

12.4   CONCLUSION

It is hoped that enough has been said in these pages to demonstrate that there is a place for the private contractor as well as the DLO in the grounds maintenance programme, and

that with careful and skilled management, each may comple-
ment the other. There is no room for complacency in today's
highly competitive world, and whether we like it or not, there
is little doubt that privatization is here to stay. It should be seen
not as a threat, but as an opportunity to enable us to improve
still further the efficiency of our grounds maintenance organizations. By so doing, we shall be rendering the best possible
service to our employers, to the public and to ourselves.

The Milton Keynes Specification

The following pages contain an example of the sort of Specification that can be prepared in house using the methods outlined in Chapters 5 and 6. This Specification, with minor amendments, is typical of that which has been in use by The Milton Keynes Development Corporation for the past ten years for maintenance contracts up to the annual value of about £80 000.

The example shown was prepared for an area of housing-associated landscape on three adjoining estates and is readily adapted for any similar type of contract by altering the names, dates, quantities etc. as appropriate.

It will be noted that this document does not include any Bills of Quantities and this is normal for the type and size of maintenance contracts raised by this Authority. The contract is let on the basis of the bottom line figure only and is a fixed-price term contract relating to the quantities listed in the landscape schedule(s). Any variations or additional works are dealt with on a separate order basis as they occur and are priced according to a schedule of rates which the successful tenderer is required to price.

In the event that contracts of much greater value were to be raised it might be considered appropriate to include priced Bills in the make-up of the contract document, but with contracts up to the value of £70 000–£80 000 per annum, this has not so far been considered necessary.

Milton Keynes Development Corporation.
Landscape Maintenance Contract Section.

467

FISHERMEAD
OLDBROOK
and SPRINGFIELD
LANDSCAPE MAINTENANCE

S P E C I F I C A T I O N

FOR

LANDSCAPE MAINTENANCE WORK

at   FISHERMEAD/OLDBROOK/SPRINGFIELD

for the

M I L T O N   K E Y N E S   D E V E L O P M E N T
C O R P O R A T I O N

CONTRACT NO.   LMCS/467

MILTON KEYNES DEVELOPMENT CORPORATION

RECREATION UNIT

7 North Tenth Street
Central Milton Keynes
MK9 3DU

PRELIMINARIES, TERMS AND CONDITIONS, SPECIFICATIONS AND SCHEDULE

FOR WORKS TO BE EXECUTED IN CONNECTION WITH A CONTRACT FOR

LANDSCAPE MAINTENANCE WORK IN MILTON KEYNES NEW TOWN IN THE

COUNTY OF BUCKINGHAMSHIRE FOR THE MILTON KEYNES DEVELOPMENT

CORPORATION FOR THE PERIOD:

FROM 1 APRIL 1989 TO 31 MARCH 1991

BILL NO. 1 - PRELIMINARIES

BILL NO. 2 - GENERAL CONDITIONS

BILL NO. 3 - SPECIFICATION

APPENDIX A - HEDGE CATEGORIES

B - LANDSCAPE SCHEDULE

C - LANDSCAPE DEPOTS

D - HIGH MAINTENANCE AREAS

E - BASIC PROTECTIVE CLOTHING

F - DRAWINGS

G - NOTES ON GRASSCUTTING

CONTRACT NO.: LMCS/467   DATE: 11 OCTOBER 1988

BILL NO. 1

PRELIMINARIES

1.1 SCOPE OF CONTRACT

a) The proposed Contract is to run from

1 April 1989 to 31 March 1991

and will include for :

The routine general landscape maintenance and litter collection of the areas within the Contract boundary for the total Contract period.

The main operations required will be grass cutting and edging, tree, shrub and hedge maintenance including pruning and weed control, litter collection and weed control of gravel and hard surfaces.

b) Other landscape work of a similar nature may be ordered as required, and such work will be paid for additionally to the overall Contract sum, in accordance with the Schedule of Rates (see Clause 2.19).

c) The Employer may, subject to the receipt of a satisfactory tender and satisfactory progress of the works, negotiate with the successful tenderer for a further period of up to two years.

The basis for negotiation will be this Contract, adjusted to meet conditions at the time of negotiation.

1.2 NAMES OF PARTIES DEFINITIONS AND ABBREVIATIONS

"The Employer" shall be the Milton Keynes Development Corporation, Saxon Court, 502 Avebury Boulevard, Central Milton Keynes, MK9 3HS.

"The Contractor" shall be the successful tenderer, appointed by the Employer.

"The Supervising Officer" shall be Mr D.R. Hopkins, Manager, Landscape Contract Maintenance.

The term "Supervising Officer" wherever used in the contract documents, shall be deemed to include his authorised representatives.

Site/Maintenance Area - The total area of landscaped ground within the contract boundary. See Clauses 1.3 and 1.4 and the drawings provided.

Fine grass areas - Established grass areas with smooth surfaces, free from bumps and hollows with no loose stones or similar objects on its surface, and with well defined edges. Suitable for close mowing using cylinder type machines.

3

Rough grass areas - Grass areas with rough or uneven
surface, sometimes with loose stones on the surface.
Indeterminate and loosely defined edges. Areas which
are often littered. Usually unsuitable for cylinder
mowing, should be cut with rotary or flail type machines
after removal of stones and litter.

Hard Surfaces - Those hard surfaces within the Contract
Area, included in the Landscape Schedule and marked on the
Drawings, which require to be kept clean and weedfree
within the terms of the Contract.
They may include paving, brickwork, blockwork, tarmacadam,
loose gravel and the like.
The Contractor should note that the adopted Public Highway
is excluded from the maintenance requirements of this
Contract.

Litter - horticultural residues and arisings, paper,
bottles, cans, broken glass and all other extraneous
objects and materials whatsoever their composition and by
whomsoever deposited.

Abbreviations:

S.O. - Supervising Officer

mm   - millimetre(s) m^2 - square metre(s)

cm   - centimetre(s)   ha - hectare(s)

 m   - metre(s)   g - gramme(s)

1.3   LOCATION OF AND ACCESS TO THE MAINTENANCE AREA

The maintenance area is situated at

Fishermead, Oldbrook and Springfield

as shown on the location plan on the last page of this
document.

Access to the maintenance area shall be by public roads as
shown on the drawings provided. The Contractor will be
responsible for ensuring that his own vehicles and those of
subcontractors, suppliers or others employed in the
maintenance, use only the agreed routes.

1.4   LIMITATIONS OF THE MAINTENANCE AREA

The limit of the Contractors maintenance area is shown on
the drawings listed in Appendix 'F'.

The Contractor should note that some of the site boundaries
may not be defined by existing physical features.

4

1.5   PRELIMINARY INVESTIGATION

   a) The tenderer shall visit the Contract Site in the
      company of the S.O. or his representative and shall
      satisfy himself of the full requirements of the
      Contract, prior to the submission of his Tender. He
      shall carry out any investigations that he may consider
      necessary to satisfy himself of the ground conditions,
      the availability of water and electricity for any
      temporary supplies that may be required in carrying out
      the works, the extent, character and accessibility of
      the site and all other conditions affecting the works,
      prevailing at the time of his inspection.

   b) The Tenderer shall satisfy himself as to the supply of,
      and conditions affecting, labour and all local
      conditions and shall allow for all costs and expenses
      incurred in maintaining an adequate and effective labour
      force on the works.

   c) No claim on the grounds of lack of knowledge of any of
      the above mentioned items will be entertained.

1.6   DECLARATION OF INTEREST

   The Contractor agrees that neither he nor any Director if a
   limited company nor any Partner or Employee is related to
   any Member or Employee of the Employer nor that any Member
   or Employee of the Corporation has any interest whether
   financial, managerial or otherwise in the Contractor other
   than any such relationship or interest communicated in
   writing to the Employer prior to the date of the Tender.

BILL NO. 2

GENERAL CONDITIONS

2.1 STANDARD OF WORK

a) All operations shall be undertaken in a professional and workmanlike manner in accordance with the principles of good horticultural practice and the standard of the finished works shall be in keeping with this requirement and to the satisfaction of the S.O.

b) It should be noted that on some sites certain areas have been designated as "high maintenance areas".
These are to receive a higher standard of maintenance compared to the rest of the site with greater attention paid to all operations and greater frequency of visits. (See Appendix D and Appendix G).

The tenderer should allow for this extra work, if applicable, when compiling his Tender.

2.2 LABOUR

The Contractor shall provide all skilled and unskilled labour necessary for the due completion of the works.

2.3 COMPETENT PERSON

The Contractor shall ensure that a Foreman, Chargehand or other competent person shall be present on site at all times when the works are in hand. Such competent person shall be capable and authorised to accept day to day instructions from the S.O. concerning the works in hand and to ensure that they are effectively carried out by the personnel under his charge.

2.4 WEEKEND WORKING

If the Contractor wishes to work on Saturdays after midday, Sundays or Bank Holidays, prior notice must be given and permission obtained from the S.O. Where sub-contractors are used on the works, the Contractor must ensure that they are aware of and conform to this requirement.

2.5   EXCLUSION FROM THE WORKS

The S.O. may (but not unreasonably or vexatiously) issue instructions requiring the exclusion from the works of any person employed thereon.

2.6   PLANT AND TOOLS

a) The Contractor shall provide all tools, plant, equipment, transport, fuel and other appliances required for the proper completion of the works in a good and workmanlike manner to the true intent and meaning of this Specification.

b) All tools, materials, plant and equipment used on the works will be used in a workmanlike manner and will comply with all appropriate legal and safety requirements.

2.7   MATERIALS

a) The Employer shall supply materials including tree stakes and ties, trees, shrubs, plants and seeds, fertilizers, and the like for use on the maintenance area.   There shall be no charge to the Contractor for these materials.
The Contractor shall collect materials for use on the maintenance area from time to time, and as required, from the Employer's nursery in Milton Keynes.
The cost of such collections, storage and distribution to site shall be borne by the Contractor.   The Contractor shall notify the S.O. of his requirements for materials as and when the need arises.
The S.O. will then issue the necessary authority for their collection.   No materials will be issued without such authority.
The Contractor should ensure that all materials issued to him are in good condition.

b) The Contractor shall supply herbicides and dye for use on the maintenance area.   There shall be no separate payment for the supply of these materials and the Contractor shall be deemed to have allowed for their cost in his Tender.
The herbicides required shall be contact, translocated and residual herbicides in liquid, granulated or powdered form.
The quantity of herbicide supplied shall be such as is necessary to maintain an adequate level of weed control in accordance with the Specification throughout the maintenance area.
Only herbicide approved under the Control of Pesticides Regulations 1986 shall be supplied.

2.8   WATER SUPPLY

Should water be necessary for any work the Contractor is to make his own arrangement for such supply of water.   The water undertaking covering the whole of the sites included in this Contract is Anglian Water.

2.9   CLEANING UP

The Contractor shall clear away all rubbish and debris from
all operations as the work proceeds. Earth, grass cuttings
and rubbish shall not be allowed to remain on footways.
Any excavations shall be effectively covered and
arrangements made for any watching or lighting necessary.
All areas are to be left clean and tidy on completion of
each day's work. On completion of the Contract the
Contractor shall remove all structures used in connection
with the works, clean up and leave the site in a clean and
tidy condition and make good any damage.

2.10   PROVISION OF TIP

a) The Contractor shall be responsible for the provision of
   a tipping facility and for ensuring that all rubbish is
   removed thereto. Such facility shall be off site and no
   unauthorised tipping shall be carried out within the
   Maintenance Area or in any other place.

b) All charges, fees, transport and other expenses in
   connection with tipping shall be borne by the Contractor.

c) Rubbish skips will not be used on site except with the
   written permission of the S.O. If such permission is
   given the siting of the skips shall be as agreed with
   the S.O. prior to their use.

2.11   HEALTH AND SAFETY ACT

a) All operations shall be performed having due regard to
   the regulations and provisions of the Health and Safety
   at Work Act, 1974.

b) The Contractor shall provide the following minimum
   facilities in all caravans, mobile depots and/or
   vehicles from which the operatives work:

   i)   A supply of fresh water for washing purposes, in a
        suitable container, of at least five gallons
        capacity, with a tap.
   ii) Soap, paper towels and a bowl for washing.
   iii) First Aid box appropriate to the size of the gang
        and the nature of the work.

c) The Contractor shall nominate a member of his staff to
   be responsible for safety, health and welfare and such
   nominated person shall liaise with the Employer's
   Personnel Officer, via the S.O., on all relevant
   occasions throughout the duration of the Contract.

d) Adequate protective measures shall be taken to protect
   employees, members of the public and all other persons.

e) The Contractor's attention is drawn to Appendix E –
   BASIC PROTECTIVE CLOTHING with which he is required to
   comply on all relative occasions.

8

f) Where an accident occurs on site which is notifiable to
H.M. Factory Inspectorate under the Reporting of
Injuries, Diseases and Dangerous Occurences Regulations
1985, a copy of the notification shall be given to the
S.O., who will inform the Employer's Personnel Officer.

2.12 FIRE PRECAUTIONS

The Contractor shall take all reasonable precautions to
minimise fire risks and shall conform to such instructions
as may be given to him from time to time by the S.O.

2.13 DAMAGE TO LANDSCAPE FEATURES

The Contractor will be held responsible for any damage to
trees, shrubs, hedges, grass or other soft or hard
landscape features caused by his acts or his negligence.
In the case of minor superficial damage the Contractor
shall carry out such remedial measures as the S.O. shall
direct. The Employer reserves the right, in all cases, to
make alternative arrangements for the rectification of such
damage, using his own or any other Agency.

2.14 DAMAGE TO HIGHWAYS ETC.

The Contractor will be held responsible for any damage to
the highways, roads, kerbs, channels, footpaths, pavements,
services, etc. caused by his acts or his negligence and he
shall make good any such damage as may be caused at his own
expense. The Contractor is to include for keeping the
roadways, pavements and footpaths clear of soil, mud, grass
cuttings and other obstructions to the satisfaction of the
Local Highways Authority and the Employer.

2.15 CONTRACTORS LIABILITY

a) The Contractor shall keep in force throughout the
Contract period an insurance policy covering him against
third party claims for injury (including fatal injury)
or damage to persons or property in the sum of at least
£1,000,000 for any one occurrence or series of
occurrences arising out of one event, and shall procure
the endorsement on the policy of the Employer's interest
therein. Any such policy and the receipt for current
premiums shall on demand be produced to the Employer for
inspection.

b) The Employer shall not be liable for any claims in
respect of injury (including fatal injury) or damages
arising out of or in connection with the execution of
this Contract to any person or property unless such
injuries or damages shall be caused by any act or
neglect of the Employer or his servants.

9

2.16 ENTRY ON OCCUPIED PREMISES

Houses in the area covered by this Contract are occupied.
Before entering any occupied premises to undertake any work
included in this Contract due notice must be given to and
permission obtained from such occupier.

2.17 LANDSCAPE DEPOTS

a) Landscape Depots are provided on some of the maintenance
areas. These Depots are provided with mess room,
machinery store/workshop, toilets and washing facilities
and external yard. Some of them may also have a
telephone installed.

The Contractor is required to make use of such Depots as
are provided and listed in Appendix C in order to
facilitate the maintenance and to assist in meeting his
obligations under the Health and Safety at Work Act,
1974. Each Depot will command a rent of one peppercorn
(not required) per year or any portion of a year. The
tenancy will be available to the Contractor for the
duration of the Contract. The Contractor will enjoy
sole possession of each Depot which must not be used for
any purpose other than in connection with the Contract
to which it relates. No sub-letting will be allowed.

b) For each and every Depot:

The Contractor shall pay rent (as described above),
Electricity, Gas and Water charges excluding standing
charges, Telephone charges (excluding rental), and such
repairs and dilapidations as becomes necessary as a
direct result of his occupancy. Value Added Tax will be
added to all such charges as appropriate.

The Employer will pay standing charges in respect of
Electricity, Gas and Water, rental charges for telephone
General Rates, routine maintenance and such repairs as
are not directly attributable to the Contractor's use of
the premises.

The Contractor will be required to enter into a separate
tenancy agreement in respect of each Landscape Depot
that he occupies.

c) The Contractor will not be allowed to erect, construct
or use site depots, caravans, compounds or other such
facilities of his own choosing.
Where no Landscape Depot is provided for use on the
Contract use must be made of publicly available
facilities and the Contractor's attention is drawn to
Clause 2.11 b).

2.18 VALUE ADDED TAX

All prices quoted shall be exclusive of value added tax.

10

In order to satisfy the requirements of H.M. Customs and
Excise the Contractor will supply a pro-forma at the
commencement of each contract year to cover the whole of
the V.A.T. due on the total contract price for that year.
The Employer will then add the appropriate amount of V.A.T.
to each payment as it becomes due.

2.19   SCHEDULE OF RATES FOR ADDITIONAL WORK

a) The successful tenderer shall be required to complete a
   Schedule of Rates for individual items of work relevant
   to the type of work embraced by this contract.

b) The Employer may wish to authorise additional work in
   connection with this contract during the contract period
   over and above that which is required under the stated
   terms. Such additional work may be offered in the first
   instance to the Contractor and paid according to the
   rates quoted in his Schedule of Rates.

c) Any additional work authorised under the clause shall be
   separately ordered and paid for and shall not be
   included in the Contract Price unless a Variation Order
   has been made in accordance with Clause 2.21.

   The Contractor has the right to refuse such offers of
   additional work without prejudice to his rights under
   any other term of the contract.

   The Employer does not guarantee that any additional work
   will be offered and reserves the right to offer such
   additional work as is required to any other contractor.

2.20   FLUCTUATIONS

The tendered price and rates quoted in the Schedule of
Rates shall not be subject to any fluctuations in respect
of changes in the rates of wages or prices of materials or
other variations whatsoever during the currency of the
Contract except as in accordance with Clause 2.22.

2.21   VARIATIONS

The Employer may from time to time issue variation orders
which may increase or decrease the amount of regular work
required under the Contract.
The value of such variation orders will be calculated by
reference to the Contractor's Schedule of Rates and the
agreed amount will be applied as an adjustment to the
Contract Price for the purpose of all subsequent payments.
The total value of all such variations in any one year
shall not exceed 10% of the Contract Price.

2.22   ADJUSTMENT OF CONTRACT PRICE

On each anniversary of the date for the return of Tenders
the Contract Price will be adjusted to take account of

11

fluctuations in the cost of labour and fuel. Such
adjustment shall be made by increasing or decreasing: a)
The Schedule of Rates and b) The Contract Price divided by
three years, by 80% of the increase or decrease in the
Government's Price Adjustment Indices as calculated by the
Property Services Agency and published by HMSO between the
month prior to the date for the return of the Tenders and
the month prior to the anniversary.

If for any reason the Price Indices are not published or
their publication is delayed then the Employer shall
calculate substitute indices on a fair and reasonable basis.

If prior to the issue of the Final Certificate publication
of the Indices is resumed or otherwise becomes available
adjustment shall be made in the next Interim Certificate or
the Final Certificate as if publication had not ceased or
been delayed.

2.23 CERTIFICATES

a) At the end of each calendar month after the Contractor
   has commenced work and providing that the Contractor has
   satisfactorily completed that portion of the works due
   up to that time, the Employer will issue an Interim
   Certificate. Such Interim Certificate will authorise
   payments from the Employer to the Contractor in respect
   of work performed by the Contractor under the Contract
   since the issue of the last preceeding Certificate.

b) At the end of the Contract Period and providing that all
   works due under the terms of the Contract have been
   satisfactorily completed the Employer will issue a Final
   Certificate. Such Final Certificate will authorise
   payment from the Employer to the Contractor of the
   balance of monies due to the Contractor under the terms
   of this Contract.

c) The Employer reserves the right to delay the issue of
   any Certificate or to withhold all or part of any
   payment in cases where the works are incomplete or
   unsatisfactory. The decision as to whether the works
   are complete and satisfactory shall be that of the S.O.
   whose decision on the matter shall be final.

d) In the event of any Certificate being withheld or
   purposefully delayed the Contractor shall be informed in
   writing of the reason for such action within seven days
   of the due date of the Certificates.

2.24 PAYMENTS

a) Payment shall be made by the Employer to the Contractor
   on the issue of Interim and Final Certificates as
   described in Clause 2.23.

12

b) The value of such Interim Certificates shall be the Contract Price divided by three years and adjusted in accordance with Clause 2.22, divided by the number of months in the current Contract Year, normally one twelth, and subsequent to increase or decrease by the proportionate amount of any Variation Orders which may have been made in the current Contract Year.

c) In the event that the work is not commenced during the first month or months of the Contract Period the amount due in the first Contract Year as calculated in accordance with Sub Clause (b) above will be divided by the number of months remaining in the Contract Year.

2.25 RECTIFICATION OF WORK

During the period of one calendar month following the end of the Contract Period and at any time during the Contract Period the Contractor may be required to rectify any outstanding works required under the terms of the Contract. Such rectification and completion shall be at the Contractor's expense. Failure of the Contractor to carry out such work to the satisfaction of the S.O. may result in the Employer making alternative arrangements to complete the Contract works using his own or any other Agency. In such cases the cost of the alternative arrangements shall be deducted from any monies due to the Contractor. Any balance shall be a debt recoverable by action from the Contractor.

2.26 ASSIGNMENT AND SUB-LETTING

a) By Contractor

The Contractor shall not, without the written consent of the Employer assign this Contract, and shall not without the written consent of the S.O. (which shall not unreasonably be withheld to the prejudice of the Contractor) sub-let any portion of the works.

It shall be a condition in any sub-letting which may occur that the employment of the subcontractor under the sub-contract shall determine immediately upon the determination (for any reason) of the Contractor's employment under this Contract.

b) By Employer

It is possible that the Employer may wish to transfer his interests in this Contract to another party. Such assignment is not imminent but may become so at some future date. The Employer reserves the right to assign all the Employers rights, duties and benefits to another responsible party and the Contractor agrees to such assignment subject to the following conditions :

     i)   The Employer shall consult with the Contractor at the earliest practicable time if assignment becomes imminent.

    ii)   The Contract shall continue in force before during and after negotiations for assignment with no break in continuity of the work.

    iii)   No changes shall be made in the terms and conditions of the contract except those changes that are considered necessary for administrative purposes. Any changes that are made shall be not less favourable to the Contractor than those existing before the assignment.

    iv)   At some time prior to the date of assignment the Contractor will have the right to meet with the assignee to discuss the effects of the assignment.

    v)   In the event that the Contractor is unable to agree to the proposals for assignment of the Contract he shall have the right to refer the matter to arbitration as in Clause 2.31.

2.27. CORPORATION PROPERTY

The Contractor guarantees the due return of all the Employer's property issued to him and will be responsible to the full value of such property, to be assessed by the Employer for all loss or damage from whatever cause happening thereto while in the possession or control of himself, his servants or agents.

2.28. RECOVERY OF SUMS DUE

Whenever under this Contract any sum of money shall be recoverable from or payable by the Contractor, the same may be deducted from any sum then due or which at any time thereafter may become due to the Contractor under this Contract.

2.29 TAX CERTIFICATE

The Contractor shall be in possession of a valid Subcontractor's Tax Certificate (Form 714C, P or I) and shall produce it for inspection by the Employer when required to do so.

2.30 DETERMINATION

By the Employer

The Employer may in writing determine the Contract (but without prejudice to the rights of the parties accrued to the date of determination) in any of the following cases:

14

    i)   Default: If the Contractor, having been given notice by the S.O. to re-execute work which has not been performed in accordance with the Specification, or to proceed with the work in such a manner as to enable completion to be effected by the date named, fails within a reasonable time to comply with such notice.

       The period of time regarded as reasonable for the purpose of this clause shall be stated in the notice.

   ii)   Corrupt Gifts: If the Contractor or anyone employed by him or acting on his behalf shall commit an offence under the Prevention of Corruption Acts 1889 to 1916 in relation to this or any other Contract with the Employer.

  iii)   Upon any breach of Clause 1.6.

   iv)   Bankruptcy: If the Contractor becomes bankrupt or makes any composition or arrangement with his creditors or has a winding-up order made or (except for the purpose of reconstruction) a resolution for voluntary winding-up passed or a receiver or manager of his business or undertaking is duly appointed or possession is taken by or on behalf of any creditor of any property the subject of a charge.

In the event of the determination of the Contract as aforesaid the Employer may either by use of his own employees or by the employment of any other Contractor or Contractors complete the works or any part thereof and recover the excess cost from the Contractor.

  b) By the Contractor

    The Contractor may in writing determine the Contract (but without prejudice to the rights of the parties accrued to the date of determination) in any of the following cases:

     i)   Payments: If the Employer fails to make any payment due under the provisions of Clause 2.24 within 28 days of the issue of the Certificate.

    ii)   Obstruction: If the Employer or any person for whom he is responsible interferes with or obstructs the carrying out of the works to the detriment of the maintenance standard and to the financial disadvantage of the Contractor.

2.31   ARBITRATION

    If any dispute of difference concerning this Contract shall arise between the Employer or S.O. on his behalf and the Contractor, such dispute shall be referred to the arbitration and final decision of a person to be agreed between the parties, or failing agreement within 14 days after either party has given the other a written request to concur in the appointment of an arbitrator, a person to be appointed on the request of either party by the President or Vice President for the time being of the Landscape Institute.

15

<u>BILL NO. 3</u>

<u>SPECIFICATION OF THE WORKS</u>

3.1 <u>PRINCIPAL OPERATIONS</u>

The principal operations required will be grass cutting,
including edging, tree maintenance, herbicide applications
to shrub beds, trees, hedges and hard surfaces, pruning of
shrubs, trees and hedges, hedge cutting and general litter
collection. Other operations of a less general nature will
be required according to the dictates of normal good
horticultural practice and the requirements of the site.
These may include handweeding, pest and disease control,
minor reinstatement works and the like.
All such operations shall form part of the normal contract
works and the Contractor shall be deemed to have allowed
for such items in his Tender, but see Clause 1.1 b).

3.2 <u>TIMING OF OPERATIONS</u>

a) The Employer reserves the right to vary, adjust or
   extend the timing of specific operations to take account
   of site conditions and seasonal variations.

b) The timing of specific operations shall be as stated in
   the contract unless otherwise agreed with the S.O.

c) The timing of specific operations where not stated in
   the contract shall be as the S.O. directs.

3.3 <u>HERBICIDE APPLICATION</u>

a) All herbicides and chemicals used shall be those agreed
   with the Employer and no other chemical shall be used.

b) the Contractor will inform the S.O. a minimum of 48
   hours and a maximum of 7 days prior to each intended
   application of herbicide and detail the locations to be
   treated. The Employer reserves the right to defer the
   operations, or to suspend it if in progress, if in the
   opinion of the S.O., the work is thought likely to be
   dangerous or damaging to the site, plant material or
   members of the public.

c) The Contractor shall be responsible for the safe and
   proper storage and application of any herbicide he shall
   use and shall comply with all relevant legislation,
   Statutory Instruments and Codes of Practice.
   Herbicide and dye will not be left unattended unless
   placed in a securely locked box.

16

d) All persons employed on the handling and use of herbicides shall wear basic protective clothing in accordance with the requirements of Appendix E.

e) In accordance with the Control of Pesticides Regulations 1986 all herbicide operators shall hold Certificates of Competence appropriate to the type of operation in progress or shall work under the direct and personal supervision of a holder of such a Certificate or Certificates at all times. Currently not more than three non-certificated operatives shall work under the responsibility of a Certificate holder and from 1 January 1990 not more than two.

The Employer may require to inspect Certificates of Competence at any reasonable times and may suspend herbicide operations immediately in the event of Certificated personnel being not present on site when herbicide application is in progress.

f) The Contractor shall supply approved signs stating "Herbicide Application in Progress". Sufficient signs will be erected by the Contractor before work commences to ensure that, as far as is reasonably practicable, members of the public are made aware that herbicide application is being, or is about to be, undertaken. All such signs shall remain in position throughout the operation and shall be removed immediately it has been completed.

g) Dilution rates and rates of application of all chemicals shall be those specified by the Employer.

h) All bottles, tins, bags, wrappers or other form of container which have contained chemicals, shall when empty, be disposed of in a safe and proper manner.

i) All spray equipment shall be efficient, well maintained and free from leaks. The type of herbicide, type and size of spray nozzle, knapsack pressure, dilution and rate of application will be appropriate to the herbicide and site of application and must be agreed with the S.O. before application commences.

j) Great care must be taken to ensure that no damage is done to shrubs, trees, bulbs or other planted material or grass surfaces, whether owned by the Employer, residents, or other parties. To this end, maximum precautions must be taken to obtain accurate placement of herbicides, avoiding drift.

k) Spraying must not take place during windy or otherwise unsuitable weather conditions. Particular care will be taken to avoid damaging species with green or otherwise sensitive bark.

17

l) The application of granular herbicide shall be made by
means of an approved spreader.

m) The use of blue marker dye may occasionally be required
by the Employer. The S.O. will indicate his
requirements where this applies.
Where marker dye is used it shall be of a type that is
compatible with the herbicide with which it is mixed.

The handling and storage of marker dye shall be subject to
the same requirements as with herbicides already described.

3.4 PRUNING

a) the regular pruning of all trees and shrubs shall be
carried out in order to attain the following objectives:

  i)   To promote new growth.

  ii) To increase the potential for future flowering/
       fruiting.

  iii) To maintain and improve health by removal of dead
       and diseased wood.

  iv) To avoid undue damage to adjacent plants and
       maintain the balance of species.

  v)   To prevent obstruction of sight lines at traffic
       corners and junctions.

  vi) To prevent encroachment on roads, paths and
       walkways.

  vii) To prevent obstruction of light to windows of
       buildings.

b) Pruning shall be carried out by skilled labour only.

c) All prunings, dead plants and other debris shall be
gathered up, collected and removed from site, at the
conclusion of each day's work. The Contractor will be
responsible for providing his own tipping facility.

d) All dead wood shall be cut out cleanly and suckers
removed and the plants pruned, trimmed, thinned out,
shaped and tied in at the appropriate time, as necessary
according to kind, species and variety in order to
achieve objective i) - iv) above.

e) Shrubs and other plants must not be allowed to grow out
across paths, roads or cycleways so as to cause a hazard
to pedestrians or vehicles. Particular attention will
be paid to road junctions and places where footpaths and
cycleways cross or meet roads and redways.

18

f) i.   Shrubs and trees shall not be allowed to grow in
        front of windows of buildings in a manner such as
        to cause obstruction of light.

   ii. All shrubs which in the opinion of the S.O. have
        exceeded the intended stature shall be reduced in
        height and/or spread or in extreme cases removed
        completely as the S.O. directs.

g) Climbing plants shall be tied in and any wires, frames
   or supports inspected and repaired if necessary.

   This work shall be done at the time of pruning and at
   other times when the growth of the plants makes it
   necessary and/or when damage has occurred.

h) The Contractor shall perform all the work described in
   this Clause as part of his normal duties under the
   Contract and such items will not qualify for additional
   payment under the Terms of Clause 2.19.

3.5   <u>GRASS CUTTING</u>

a) The Contractor shall carry out all necessary preliminary
   inspections of the areas to be cut on each occasion, and
   remove isolated items of obstruction which might damage
   plant or create a possible hazard to persons or property.

b) All grassed areas shall be mowed with appropriate
   machines to produce a standard of finish in keeping with
   the particular use of the area. In general, cylinder
   type mowers shall be used wherever practical on fine
   grass areas with the exception of steep banks which may
   require small rotary mowers for practical
   considerations. Rough grass may be cut with rotary or
   flail mowers.

c) Cutters to all mowers shall be sharp and properly set
   and cut the sward cleanly and evenly.
   Mowers should have their height of cut so adjusted that
   at no time does "scalping" take place. In periods of
   prolonged drought the grass shall be left after cutting
   with a height of not less than 2 cms.

d) All fine grass areas shall be cut between the months of
   April and October inclusive so that at no time is the
   grass allowed to grow above a height of 5 cm.
   Additionally one cut will be made to all fine grass
   areas in March. (See also Appendix G - "Notes on
   Grasscutting" - Note 2).

e) All rough grass areas shall be cut between the months of
   April and October inclusive so that at no time is the
   grass allowed to grow above a height of 10cm.
   Additionally one cut will be made to all rough grass
   areas in March. (See also Appendix G - "Notes on
   Grasscutting" - Note 3)

19

f) All high maintenance grass areas shall be cut between the months of April and October inclusive so that at no time is the grass allowed to grow above a height of 4 cm. Additionally on cut will be made to all high maintenance grass areas in March. (See also Appendix G - "Notes on Grasscutting" - Note 1).

g) Where bulbs are present in grass cutting areas the above cutting regimes shall be postponed by agreement with the S.O. until such time as the S.O. requires normal cutting to commence (normally June). The areas affected shall be only that part of the grass area where bulbs are present. The arisings from the first cut shall be collected and removed to tip.

h) The contractor shall maintain to the fine grass standard (see subclause (d) above) all grass adjacent to footpaths, roads and redways to a distance of 1m from the edge of the kerb or path edging. This shall apply irrespective of whether or not such grass strips are indicated on the drawings provided.

i) Grass against walls and fences, around trees, lamp columns and other street furniture and in corners inaccessible to the normal mowers, shall be controlled by chemical means or by trimming as directed by the S.O. Such direction is likely to favour chemical treatment wherever the S.O. considers it safe and practical. Such treatment shall consist of two applications per year, using a liquid or granular herbicide. Where the S.O. considers it undesirable to apply chemicals for this purpose (e.g. grass areas separated from a resident's planted garden by an open fence) he will direct that trimming shall take place. Such trimming shall be by hand or approved mechanical means, to the same height as that left by mowing, and shall be required on each occasion that mowing takes place.

j) Grass clippings shall be spread out evenly to prevent damage to the grass beneath. Grass clippings should not be allowed to lie on paths, roads, drives and the like, but should be swept up and scattered evenly on adjoining grass areas.
Where density of grass clippings are regarded by the S.O. as detrimental, these shall be removed from site by the Contractor.

k) In addition to these specifications, the application of herbicide shall be used to maintain an area of bare earth around trees and shrubs, lamp columns, service installation markers, and along walls, fences and other hard features occurring in all grass areas included within the Contract, to a distance sufficient to enable mowing to proceed conveniently around them. (See also Clause 3.7c)

20

3.6   GRASS EDGING

All grass areas adjacent to hard surfaces shall be
maintained with clean firm edges to prevent encroachment.
This effect may be obtained by any suitable means including
chemical screefing.

All grass edges shall be inspected and any necessary edging
carried out during the month of April. Additionally, At
the end of the normal grasscutting season and within six
weeks of the final cut all such edges shall be trimmed to
clean straight lines and smooth curves using an edging iron
or its mechanical equivalent. All arisings shall be
removed as the work proceeds.

3.7   TREE MAINTENANCE

a) All planted trees ranging from whips to semi-mature
   shall be inspected twice per year in the months of
   April/May and September/October and appropriate remedial
   action taken as required.

   i)   Check base of tree for "rocking" and "socketing".
         Straighten tree, re-stake, fill voids with top soil
         and firm up, as required.

   ii)   Check tree ties. Adjust, refix or replace as
         necessary.

   iii) Check tree stakes for firmness, vertical position,
         signs of rot or damage. Refirm, remove or replace
         if necessary.

   iv)   Check tree for signs of damage to stem, crown or
         branches. Cut back broken branches. Prune to
         shape if necessary.

   v)   If dead or severely damaged, remove tree and stake,
         make good ground.

b) Additionally to above, all trees shall be similarly
   inspected and any work found to be necessary carried
   out, immediately after periods of high wind or storm
   conditions, or when vandalism or other damage has been
   reported, throughout the period of the Contract.

c) The bases of all trees shall be maintained in a weed
   free condition. Trees growing in grass areas shall be
   spot weeded to a diameter of 1m with herbicides applied
   by an approved method in order to avoid damage to the
   trees or surrounding grass. Such applications will
   consist of a liquid spray applied during the months of
   May to August and a granular herbicide during the months
   of January to March.
   (See also Clause 3.3)

21

3.8 <u>MATURE</u> <u>TREES</u> <u>AND</u> <u>HEDGES</u>

The maintenance of large mature trees and old agricultural hedges shall be excluded from the Contract and the Contractor shall not be required to carry out any work or inspections of these items other than reporting any obvious signs of damage to the S.O., should it come to his attention during the course of his normal duties. (But see Clause 3.11).

3.9 <u>SHRUB</u> <u>MAINTENANCE</u>

a) The Contractor shall maintain all shrub beds in a weed free condition. This may be achieved by a combination of hand weeding and the use of approved chemical herbicides. (See also Clause 3.3).

b) All beds with the exception of susceptible species shall be treated with an approved herbicide, or mixture of herbicides, in the form of a liquid spray, during the months of June to September inclusive. The exact timing of this operation shall be determined after consultation with the S.O. The spray shall be applied by knapsack spray, dribble bar, wheelbarrow or tractor mounted spray equipment.

c) All beds, with the exception of susceptible species shall be treated with an approved granular herbicide between the months of January to March inclusive. The exact timing of this operation shall be determined after consultation with the S.O.

d) Climbing plants shall be maintained with a weed free and grass free area at the base of each plant.

e) Hand weeding shall be carried out at the discretion of the Contractor or as directed by the S.O.

f) Care must be taken to avoid damage to, or disturbance of the roots of the planted material.

g) Hand weeding shall not take place in conditions of severe frost or drought.

h) All weeds, dead plants and debris resulting from a hand weeding operation shall be gathered up, collected and removed from site as the work proceeds. Adjacent paths or other surfaces shall be swept clean as the work proceeds and the site left tidy at the conclusion of each day's work.

22

3.10 HEDGE MAINTENANCE

a) The regular and routine trimming and clipping of hedges
   is to be regarded as an integral part of the
   maintenance. (But see Clause 3.8).

b) The Contractor is referred to Appendix A for a
   description of the four types of hedge and the manner in
   which they should be clipped. Care must be taken to
   treat each hedge in the manner described according to
   its type. The type of hedge is indicated on the
   drawings and listed on the Landscape Schedule.

c) All hedges are to be clipped on two occasions during the
   contract year. The first clipping will be in May and
   the second in September.

d) Hedge clipping will be carried out with appropriate hand
   or power tools. Large leaved plants such as laurel will
   be finished off with secateurs so as to avoid half cut
   leaves.

e) All hedge clippings are to be gathered up, collected and
   removed from site at the conclusion of each day's work.

f) The bases of all hedges shall be kept weed free. An
   application of an approved herbicide or mixture of
   herbicides in the form of a liquid spray shall be made
   during the months of June - September inclusive.
   Additionally an application of an approved granular
   herbicide shall be made between the months of January -
   March inclusive. Weeding, if necessary at any other
   time shall be hand weeding (See also Clause 3.3).

3.11 LITTER

The Contractor shall at all times be responsible for
keeping the whole site free from litter. This will involve
the regular collection of such items that can be picked up,
swept up, shovelled or otherwise man-handled into a sack,
wheelbarrow or suitable motor vehicle and removed from site
and this will be a regular part of the normal contract
work. Larger items such as discarded furniture and
household effects, mattresses, extensive deposits of garden
rubble etc., must be reported to the S.O., who may then
authorise their removal as additional work at appropriate
rates.

The Contractor should note that certain sites have litter
bins and these should be emptied regularly and the contents
removed from site.

The S.O. will direct the Contractor with regard to removal
from site of all classes of litter so as to make maximum
use of skips, Civic Amenity Tips and other facilities where
they occur on or near the Contract Area. Abandoned cars
will be excluded from the Contractor's area of
responsibility but must be reported to the S.O. in order
that he may arrange for their collection by the appropriate
Authority.

3.12 HARD SURFACES

The Contractor shall allow for one application of a total
and residual weed killer in the form of a liquid spray to
hard surface areas. The area to be so treated will be
found in the Landscape Schedule, Appendix 'B' of this
document. (See also Clause 3.3).

24

APPENDIX A

HEDGE CATEGORIES

The hedges included in the Landscape Schedule for this Contract are categorised according to the type of cutting required.

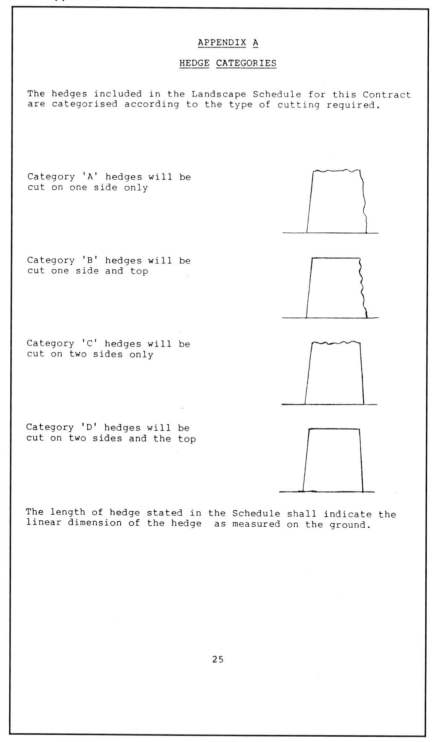

Category 'A' hedges will be cut on one side only

Category 'B' hedges will be cut one side and top

Category 'C' hedges will be cut on two sides only

Category 'D' hedges will be cut on two sides and the top

The length of hedge stated in the Schedule shall indicate the linear dimension of the hedge as measured on the ground.

25

APPENDIX B (I)

LANDSCAPE SCHEDULE

for

FISHERMEAD

These notes are for guidance only. They are intended to aid the Contractor in preparing his Tender and arranging his work programme. Although every effort has been made to ensure a reasonable standard of accuracy the Employer does not hold himself responsible for any errors of measurement or errors of omission. The Contractor should satisfy himself as to the actual areas and quantities involved and in this connection attention is drawn to clause 1.5.

No. of dwellings 1245

Area of grass	:	Fine	138,970
	:	Rough	--
		Total	138,970m^2

No. of trees	:	Whips	--
	:	Feathers	113
	:	Standards	4,268
	:	A.N.S.	1,972
	:	S.M.	290
		Total	6,643

Length of grass edging   16,620m

Length of Hedging :

Category	- A	--
	- B	500
	- C	--
	- D	440
	Total	940m

Area of shrub beds   50,150m^2

Area of Hard Surfaces   13,530m^2

Special Features :

26a

APPENDIX B (II)

LANDSCAPE SCHEDULE

for

OLDBROOK HOUSING

These notes are for guidance only. They are intended to aid the
Contractor in preparing his Tender and arranging his work
programme. Although every effort has been made to ensure a
reasonable standard of accuracy the Employer does not hold
himself responsible for any errors of measurement or errors of
omission. The Contractor should satisfy himself as to the
actual areas and quantities involved and in this connection
attention is drawn to clause 1.5.

No. of dwellings 512

Area of grass	:	Fine	72,050
	:	Rough	15,110
		Total	87,160m^2

No. of trees	:	Whips	--
	:	Feathers	2
	:	Standards	2,574
	:	A.N.S.	783
	:	S.M.	76
		Total	3,435

Length of grass edging   7,840m

Length of Hedging :

Category	- A	--
	- B	--
	- C	--
	- D	--
	Total	NIL

Area of shrub beds   29,260m^2

Area of Hard Surfaces   4,410m^2

Special Features :

26b

APPENDIX B (III)

LANDSCAPE SCHEDULE

for

OLDBROOK SHELTERED HOUSING

These notes are for guidance only. They are intended to aid the
Contractor in preparing his Tender and arranging his work
programme. Although every effort has been made to ensure a
reasonable standard of accuracy the Employer does not hold
himself responsible for any errors of measurement or errors of
omission. The Contractor should satisfy himself as to the
actual areas and quantities involved and in this connection
attention is drawn to clause 1.5.

No. of dwellings 33

Area of grass	:	Fine	1,130
	:	Rough	--
		Total	$1,130m^2$

No. of trees	:	Whips	--
	:	Feathers	--
	:	Standards	51
	:	A.N.S.	1
	:	S.M.	--
		Total	52

Length of grass edging 220m

Length of Hedging :

Category	- A	--
	- B	--
	- C	--
	- D	--
	Total	NIL

Area of shrub beds $730m^2$

Area of Hard Surfaces $380m^2$

Special Features :

26c

APPENDIX B (IV)

LANDSCAPE SCHEDULE

for

SPRINGFIELD HOUSING

These notes are for guidance only. They are intended to aid the Contractor in preparing his Tender and arranging his work programme. Although every effort has been made to ensure a reasonable standard of accuracy the Employer does not hold himself responsible for any errors of measurement or errors of omission. The Contractor should satisfy himself as to the actual areas and quantities involved and in this connection attention is drawn to clause 1.5.

No. of dwellings 595

Area of grass	:	Fine	69,050
	:	Rough	5,310
		Total	74,360m^2

No. of trees	:	Whips	--
	:	Feathers	--
	:	Standards	3,557
	:	A.N.S.	904
	:	S.M.	32
		Total	4,493m

Length of grass edging   10,270m

Length of Hedging :

Category	- A	--
	- B	2,810
	- C	--
	- D	120
	Total	2,930m

Area of shrub beds   17,270m^2

Area of Hard Surfaces   6,530m^2

Special Features :

26d

APPENDIX B (V)

LANDSCAPE SCHEDULE

for

SPRINGFIELD SHELTERED HOUSING

These notes are for guidance only. They are intended to aid the
Contractor in preparing his Tender and arranging his work
programme. Although every effort has been made to ensure a
reasonable standard of accuracy the Employer does not hold
himself responsible for any errors of measurement or errors of
omission. The Contractor should satisfy himself as to the
actual areas and quantities involved and in this connection
attention is drawn to clause 1.5.

No. of dwellings 57

Area of grass	:	Fine	6,470
	:	Rough	--
		Total	$6,470m^2$

No. of trees	:	Whips	--
	:	Feathers	--
	:	Standards	154
	:	A.N.S.	1
	:	S.M.	1
		Total	156

Length of grass edging   1,050m

Length of Hedging :

Category	- A	--
	- B	190
	- C	--
	- D	90
	Total	280m

Area of shrub beds $2,230m^2$

Area of Hard Surfaces $700m^2$

Special Features :

26e

APPENDIX <u>C</u>

<u>LANDSCAPE DEPOTS</u>

The Landscape Depot(s) available for use with this Contract
is/are situated as follows:

Rear of Fishermead Local Centre

North end of Clerkenwell Road, Springfield

and may be inspected by arrangement with the S.O. The Depots
is/are to be occupied by the Contractor under the terms of
the seperate agreement a specimen copy of which is included
with these Contract documents.

Attention is drawn to Clause 2.17.

27

<u>APPENDIX D</u>

<u>HIGH MAINTENANCE AREAS</u>

The High Maintenance Areas for this Contract are as follows
(See Clause 2.1 1b)

<u>Fishermead Local Park</u>

Area in front of the Crescent

<u>Oldbrook Sheltered Housing</u>

Areas 80, 81, 82, 83 and 84 on Drawing No. LMCS/OLD/2/4:7D

<u>Springfield Sheltered Housing</u>

Areas 25, 26, 27, 28 and 29 on Drawing No. LMCS/SP/2/1:3D

Areas 95, 96, 97, 98 and 99 on Drawing No. LMCS/SP/2/2:3E

APPENDIX E

BASIC PROTECTIVE CLOTHING

The Employer requires and the Contractor shall ensure that all of the items of protective clothing listed below shall be worn by all operatives whether directly employed by, sub-contracted to, or otherwise working for the Contractor during the whole of the time that the listed works are in progress.

a)   When using Driveall   Safety boots, safety
                                         helmet.

b)   When using Strimmers   Safety boots, face shield
                                         or goggles, long-sleeved
                                         top, long trousers.

c)   When using mowers   Safety boots, long
                                         trousers.

d)   When performing any and   Fluorescent jacket or
      all types of work on road-   waistcoat.
      side verges, roundabouts
      or central reservations

e)   When handling, using or   As detailed in Pesticide
      applying herbicides in   Policy (which see).
      concentrated or diluted
      condition

f)   When using chainsaw   Safety boots with
                                         protective guarding at
                                         front vamp and instep (or
                                         protective spats) leg
                                         protection, gloves with
                                         protective guarding on the
                                         back of the left hand,
                                         safety helmet, eye
                                         protection, ear defenders,
                                         non-snag outer clothing.

g)   When using chipping machine   Safety boots, safety
                                         helmet, eye protection,
                                         ear defenders, long
                                         sleeved non-snag outer
                                         clothing (including long
                                         trousers).

The Employer requires there to be two operatives on site at all times whilst either chainsaw or chipping machine are employed.

29

DRAWINGS

The detailed landscape drawings for this Contract are as
follows:

LMCS/OLD/2/1:7E	LMCS/OLD/2/3:7E
LMCS/OLD/2/4:7D	LMCS/OLD/2/5:7D
LMCS/OLD/2/6:7D	LMCS/SP/2/1:3D
LMCS/SP/2/2:3E	LMCS/SP/2/3:3C
LMCS/FISH/2/1:6E	LMCS/FISH/2/2:6E
LMCS/FISH/2/3:6F	LMCS/FISH/2/4:6E
LMCS/FISH/2/5:6E	LMCS/FISH/2/6:6E

Additionally, reduced scale drawings are available as follows:

LMCS/OLD/3/1:1D
LMCS/SP/3/1:1C
LMCS/FISH/3/1:1D

Copies of the drawings underlined above are included with this
Specification. If the large scale drawings listed above are
not included in this parcel they may be consulted by the
Tenderer on request, in the Contract Office. Two full sets of
detailed drawings will be supplied to the successful Tenderer
when the Contract commences.

30

APPENDIX G

NOTES ON GRASSCUTTING

1. **High Maintenance Areas.** In order to meet the Specification (page 20) it is envisaged that grass shall be cut at 9-12 day intervals with approximately 24 cuts being required in all. Weather conditions and growth rate may of course necessitate fewer or more cuts and the Tenderer should base this Tender on adherance to the height specification.

2. **Fine Grass Areas.** In order to meet the Specification (page 19) it is envisaged that grass shall be cut at 10-14 day intervals with approximately 20 cuts being required in all. Weather conditions and growth rate may of course necessitate fewer or more cuts and the Tenderer should base his Tender on adherance to the height specification.

3. **Rough Grass Areas.** In order to meet the Specification (page 19) it is envisaged that grass shall be cut at 20-30 day intervals with approximately 10 cuts being required in all. Weather conditions and growth rate may of course necessitate fewer or more cuts and the Tenderer should base his Tender on adherance to the height specification.

31

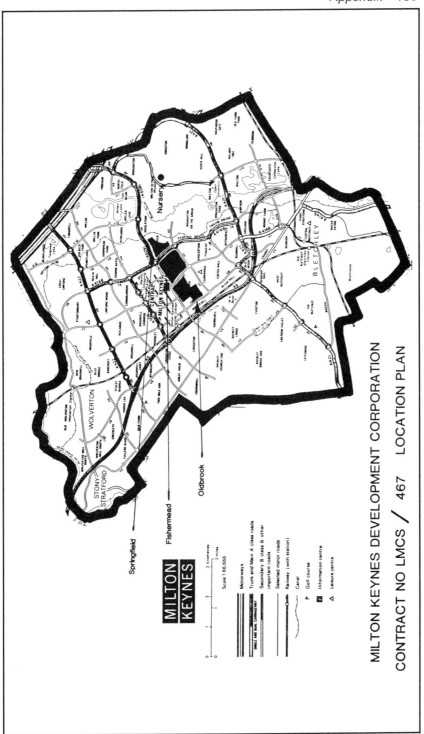

MILTON KEYNES DEVELOPMENT CORPORATION

CONTRACT NO LMCS / 467   LOCATION PLAN

Index

Page numbers in **bold** refer to figures.